Praise for *The Art of Peace*

'Experiences we thought were the preserve of far removed mystics are here poured into our laps. This succinct book makes the Divine Presence earthy. Read it.'

Ray Simpson, founding Guardian of the international Community of Aidan and Hilda

'*The Art of Peace* is like a retreat in book form. David Cole is a warm, engaging and down-to-earth writer and spiritual guide. In this book he shows us how to walk in the path of the great mystics, in our lives today. It is a lovely book.'

Carl McColman, lay Cistercian, spiritual teacher and author

The Bible Reading Fellowship
15 The Chambers, Vineyard
Abingdon OX14 3FE
brf.org.uk

The Bible Reading Fellowship (BRF) is a Registered Charity (233280)

ISBN 978 0 85746 992 2
First published 2021
10 9 8 7 6 5 4 3 2 1 0
All rights reserved

Acknowledgements
Unless otherwise acknowledged, scripture quotations are taken from The Holy
Bible, New International Version (Anglicised edition) copyright © 1979, 1984, 2011
by Biblica. Used by permission of Hodder & Stoughton Publishers, a Hachette
UK company. All rights reserved. 'NIV' is a registered trademark of Biblica.
UK trademark number 1448790.

Scripture quotations marked NCV are taken from the New Century Version®.
Copyright © 2005 by Thomas Nelson. Used by permission. All rights reserved.

Scripture quotations marked TPT are taken from The Passion Translation®.
Copyright © 2017, 2018 by Passion & Fire Ministries, Inc. Used by permission.
All rights reserved. ThePassionTranslation.com.

Scripture quotations marked NRSV are taken from The New Revised Standard
Version of the Bible, Anglicised edition, copyright © 1989, 1995 by the Division of
Christian Education of the National Council of the Churches of Christ in the United
States of America. Used by permission. All rights reserved.

Scripture quotations marked MSG are taken from *The Message*, copyright © 1993,
1994, 1995, 1996, 2000, 2001, 2002 by Eugene H. Peterson. Used by permission of
NavPress. All rights reserved. Represented by Tyndale House Publishers, Inc.

Every effort has been made to trace and contact copyright owners for material
used in this resource. We apologise for any inadvertent omissions or errors, and
would ask those concerned to contact us so that full acknowledgement can be
made in the future.

A catalogue record for this book is available from the British Library

Printed and bound by CPI Group (UK) Ltd, Croydon CR0 4YY

the art of peace

life lessons from Christian mystics

David Cole
(Brother Cassian)

Contents

'For the character of the soul is not inappropriately compared to a very light feather or plume. If it has not been harmed or spoiled by some [thing] coming from outside, thanks to its inherent lightness, it is naturally borne to the heavenly heights by the slightest breath.'

John Cassian[1]

'I [am] a feather on the breath of God.'

Hildegard of Bingen[2]

Introduction

For almost two decades I have been engaging in a daily practice of meditation and contemplation. Over those years I have also read much and studied the Christian contemplative and mystic tradition to master's degree level, and I have found that all the greatest teachings of this tradition in the Christian heritage can be summed up in the four sections you will find in this book: Stillness, Silence, Solitude and Sanctuary. These form an internal as well as external perspective.

Although my study has been a great help in gaining knowledge and inspiration about this incredibly rich tradition that I find myself in, it is the practical application on a daily basis which has really deepened my understanding and conscious awareness of what I am going to share with you. What you will read comes a little from books and head knowledge, but mostly, as all the best spiritual teachings do, from lived experience in a continually transforming life. Therefore some of what I will share has no source material other than my own experience through engagement in stillness, silence, solitude and sanctuary. I will do my best to share my experiences with you, but some things just cannot be explained by words, concepts or illustrations; one simply has to engage with this practice to experience them. In the end, the whole of the contemplative and mystic tradition is an experiential aspect to faith and spirituality. So, although I obviously encourage you to read the thoughts I share here in this book, which is a tiny drop in the vast ocean of material on this topic, I would encourage you more to get into the practice of regular (I suggest daily) contemplative mystic Christianity, as has been practised by many within our spiritual tradition over the centuries.

About 'tradition'

In a talk given in the 1980s, Professor Pelikan (a name which I always feel would beautifully suit a character in a children's television programme) differentiated between 'tradition' and 'traditionalism'. 'Tradition,' he said, 'is the living faith of the dead. Traditionalism is the dead faith of the living.'[3] That is, the rich heritage of the past can give life to those who are living out their faith today, tradition being the rich well of wisdom and knowledge that they can draw from. Traditionalism, though, is the 'it's always been done this way, so we will always do it this way' mentality that keeps things going even though they are now having a detrimental effect on those trying to live out their faith today. Pelikan went on to say, 'I suppose I should add that it is traditionalism which gives tradition a bad name. Tradition lives in conversation with the past, while remembering where we are and when we are and that it is we who have to decide.'[4] That is what I endeavour to do in this book – to live in conversation with the past, with some people who have been a great influence both on the Christian faith as a whole and on me personally and my life journey, with the intention of giving you, the reader, the ability, knowledge and perhaps even some wisdom to decide how to live in a deeper, more experiential way with the Divine.

As we journey through this book together, I will be sharing with you some things from my own lived experience and learnings, while weaving in the thoughts and wisdom of the contemplatives and mystics from throughout Christian heritage.

To find out a little more about the people I will speak of, I suggest you read my friend Carl McColman's book *Christian Mystics: 108 seers, saints, and sages*.[5] The book you hold in your hand will hopefully draw you into a place of understanding how to live a life centred on, and flowing with, the peace of God which 'transcends all understanding', as the apostle Paul puts it (Philippians 4:7), and show in practical ways how you can both *attain* and *maintain* this in the midst of the busyness of everyday life.

About 'the Divine'

You may notice that throughout this book and, in fact, in my everyday life and other writings, I refer to God more often than not as 'the Divine' rather than any other traditional term for the Christian God. There is good reason for this: words are very powerful things. The ancient druids of Britain and Ireland believed that words were so powerful that it was sacrilege to write down anything spiritual or holy, as the 'trapping' of the words on to parchment reduced their power; therefore theirs was an oral tradition. It is no coincidence that the word we use for collecting letters together to create a word and the word used for collecting words together to create 'magic' are the same word from the same root – the word 'spell', from the Proto-Germanic root *spellam*, meaning to tell or speak powerfully. The following is from an article on unity which I wrote in 2019 for the quarterly magazine of the Celtic New Monastic community that I am a vowed member of – the Community of Aidan and Hilda:[6]

> Words can be extremely divisive, they can easily exclude. Anybody who spends any time on social media will have seen, and perhaps even have experienced, the divisive power of words. But it isn't just harsh or nasty words or statements which can

cause division; people can feel excluded if words are either colloquial or jargon as well. This is true with both local dialect (which I discovered as a southerner when living in different parts of Yorkshire for a decade or so) and also that which is found within groups, including the church. Church language and jargon can be extremely exclusive. One of the reasons for this is because folk who are new to church have just never come across these words and phrases before, but another reason can also be because some people *have* been in churches, perhaps for years, and may have developed a lot of negative emotional baggage relating to certain church or religious words and language, and so the words themselves can cause a barrier for the person.

Anyone who has either read one of my books or heard me speak at or lead a retreat will probably have noticed that when I refer to the Christian deity, I tend to steer away from the word 'God'.

One of the people, or sets of people, who did notice were the editors at The Bible Reading Fellowship (BRF), who have published my last four books. Following the publication of *Celtic Advent* in 2018, I was asked to write 14 reflections on Celtic Advent for the September–December 2020 issue of *New Daylight*, one of BRF's Bible reading notes series. One of the things BRF asked was for me to explain why I steer away from the word 'God'. Here is what I wrote. I hope it helps with our understanding of unitive language:

Celtic Christianity is influencing a lot of people in the modern church, and one of the reasons for this might be that they discern something a little different from the traditional way of seeing things. This, for many, is bringing a refreshment to their spiritual lives.

You will notice that throughout my reflections I often use

the term 'Divine' rather than 'God'. This is not something one particularly finds in Celtic Christianity; rather it is from my own journey. I find that the word 'God' often has a lot of baggage for many [myself included], and that people are far too easily misled to the idea of a masculine deity when the word 'God' is used. So I more often use the term 'the Divine' when referring to the Christian deity – the whole Trinity, as the more traditional word 'God' generally means. This is why I also use a capital 'D' rather than a lower-case one, in the same way that people would write 'God' rather than 'god' when referring to the Christian deity. I have found that this is much more inclusive to folk who have struggled with the church 'God' or who have a different spiritual perspective or belief altogether.

In the same way, my prayers, rather than beginning with 'Father God' or 'Dear Lord', might begin in a more open way, similar to the manner used by Nan Merrill in her book *Psalms for Praying* (Continuum, 2007). I hope that by my slightly different semantics you find something 'more' in these devotions.

Great Divine, open my heart and mind…

About this book

Each chapter of this book will look at an aspect of the Christian contemplative or mystic tradition. With the aid of this book, the reader will be able to transition from being someone interested in, or simply practising, contemplation to *being* a contemplative. This is something which I have begun to understand is ontological rather than a verb, something where one's whole being, whole life, is, as the 20th-century Trappist monk Thomas Merton put it, 'a prolonged immersion in the rivers of tranquillity that flow from God into the whole universe and draw all things back into God'.[7]

In chapter 1 – **Slowing down** – I will be looking at the busy world we live in and giving practical ways in which we can slow down and gain a better pace of life and a balance in all we do. These will include physically slowing down, mentally slowing down and the practices of retreat and pilgrimage. This chapter will also look at the use of labyrinths.

In chapter 2 – **Be still and know** – I will be looking at the words from Psalm 46:10 and expanding on what they mean for us – what it would mean to live a life immersed in the constant cognitive awareness and total trust that God is God and 'all will be well, all things will be well, and all manner of things will be well', as Mother Julian of Norwich said.[8]

In chapter 3 – **Still here** – I will be looking at the growing interest in mindfulness and living in the constant awareness of the Divine presence at all times; being fully present in the moment and what that means from a specifically Christian perspective. This chapter will also look at the practice of Centring Prayer.

In chapter 4 – **In pursuit of silence** – I will be looking at the idea of finding silence, what silence actually is and how we cope with the noise level in the world in which we live. The title of this chapter is taken from a documentary film and will include references to it.[9]

In chapter 5 – **Into the silent land** – I will be looking at how to gain a sense of silence internally; how to still and quiet the internal conversation and dialogue which goes on constantly within ourselves. We will take some of what we learned from the previous chapter and implement it to our internal world. The title and inspiration for the material in this chapter comes from the book of the same name by Martin Laird.[10]

In chapter 6 – **The wordless way** – I will be looking at apophatic theology and the unknowing of God. We will consider prayer without words and an understanding of God without concepts.

In chapter 7 – **Go to your cell** – I will be looking at one of the specific teachings in desert monasticism and traditional monasticism, that is, to go and spend time in silence in your monastic cell or room, and in the silence discovering all that you need to know. In this chapter we will look at the concepts of both solitude and silence and at the instruction of Christ to his disciples on prayer in the sermon on the mount to go to a solitary place and use few words (Matthew 6:6–7).

In chapter 8 – **The desert of your heart** – following on from the previous chapter, I will be looking specifically at the Desert Fathers and Mothers and how we can implement their teaching and practices into our own inner lives.

In chapter 9 – **Alone together** – I will be looking at the contemplative life from a monastic perspective, focusing mostly on New Monasticism. We will look at the difference that collective silence and practising this life together with others can make.

In chapter 10 – **Seeking refuge** – I will look at the concept of seeking refuge in the Divine presence in our inner selves. We will look at verses such as Psalm 46:1, and what they can mean in our pursuit to gain and maintain the stillness and silence we have looked at so far, particularly when we feel we are in times of desolation in our contemplative practice.

In chapter 11 – **Natural space** – I will be looking at the connection to nature in the Christian tradition and the concept of quantum consciousness. We will explore engaging with the natural world in a more spiritual way.

In chapter 12 – **Contemplata aliis tradere** – I will be looking at how contemplative practice and the contemplative life can affect the world in which we are each individually called to live. *Contemplata aliis tradere* is a Latin phrase which means to pass on to others what we have gained in contemplation, and it is one of the central tenets of the Dominican Order. This chapter will look at how we can live our lives as contemplatives in an ontological context and how we can practise contemplative outreach and engage in contemplative mission simply by 'being'.

I hope that this little addition of mine to the vast ocean of wisdom on this subject will help draw you closer to, and live more deeply in, the Divine presence within you, surrounding you, saturating you and flowing through the whole universe.

Part I

Stillness

1

Slowing down

I believe the retreat as part of our normal spiritual routine will yield on the whole its fullest results when we regard it more often and more generally, in Abbot Delattes's beautiful phrase, as an opportunity of 'steeping our souls in the beauty of the mysterious'... by taking the soul from its normal pre-occupations and placing it in an atmosphere and condition which, with the minimum of distraction, it can attend to and realize God... To dwell quietly and without self-occupation in the atmosphere of God is surely the best way of all ways of redressing the balance between the temporal and eternal sides of our life... And this, in essence, is a retreat.

Evelyn Underhill[1]

We live in a busy world. In western culture the importance of 'doing' far outweighs the importance of 'being'. In fact, to many the idea of just 'being', of intentionally creating space to do nothing, would be a completely alien concept, or even, at its greatest extreme, a flagrant waste of precious time.

Over the months of the Covid-19 pandemic of 2020–21, many people were forced into a situation where they had to do much less than they were used to. Many were forced into doing nothing. The whole of the western world basically shut down for around three months, creating millions of mini monastic centres in homes across the globe, before slowly starting back up again in incremental stages over the following months. Many people found a greater appreciation for a slower and less full life. Some may have even tried to keep it. This is the type of life which has been intentionally lived by many throughout history, despite what the rest of the world is doing. These are the contemplatives, the mystics.[2] These are the ones who discover a deeper and more transcendent aspect of life interwoven with the Divine, who surrounds, saturates and penetrates everything which is – physical, metaphysical and spiritual. These people already know about the balance and rhythm of life and the importance of not being overwhelmed by what there is to do, and they understand the importance of creating space to simply 'be'.

We have many and various examples from our spiritual heritage to guide us in this different way of life. Here is a retelling of one to begin with:

It was a hot day. They were almost all hot days. He stood at the side of the lake that morning and knew that there was work to do. He had come here to give spiritual teaching. That was his job, at least at the moment, not that he had really been given a job description. He did love teaching outside, though. He looked around at the crowd of people who had come to listen to what he had to say. There were so many of them; the pressure was on. He had to get to work. But there were too many people to hear him from where he was standing, so he decided to get into a boat that was resting at the shore. He knew the owner, so it was okay. In fact, he asked the owner to get in the boat with him, to push it out a bit and keep it steady as he sat in the boat and gave the talk which he had in his head.

Later that day, he came across a man who was really quite ill. He prayed over the man and the man was healed. Obviously the man was ecstatic! He went off and told everyone in the local area about what had happened, and so that evening even more people came to hear the teachings of this man and to ask for prayer for healing. The evening crowd was even bigger than the morning one. Even more pressure was being put on to do the work which was expected. But this time the teacher responded differently. He saw the crowd, knew that they were here to listen to him and be prayed over for healing – but he knew that this time, it was time to go and not to stay. Time to 'be' and not 'do'. He would not be pressurised by the work he 'should' be doing, nor the expectations of others of what he should or ought to do, but he would do what he knew was right at this time. He would go and dwell in stillness, silence and solitude, gaining sanctuary with God. So that is what he did. He walked away from the crowd that evening. He didn't teach them anything. None of them were healed through his prayers. He left them, untaught and unhealed, and went off to a quiet place on his own, as, in fact, he often did, and spent quiet contemplative time with God.

You have probably twigged already that this is my own paraphrased retelling of the story of Jesus found at the start of Luke 5 (vv. 1–3, 12–16). It is a story, or illustration, which I use regularly when teaching on slowing down, on not being pressured by the work we have to do, the job we have been given or the expectations of others of how we should be, what we should be doing and how much we should be working. It is the perfect example of a work–life balance given to us from the life of Jesus himself. Twice in this passage Jesus is confronted by crowds who want him to do his job, to engage in his ministry. The first time Jesus does exactly that. He does his job, as it were. He sits and teaches the crowd, then heals someone. Later, however, he has a different reaction. Once again he is confronted by a crowd and expected to do his job, yet this time he doesn't do what we, or they, might expect. He knows that this time the bigger priority is for his own inner well-being. So he leaves the crowd, untaught, unhealed, and goes away on his own to find sanctuary with God in stillness, silence and solitude.

There are two words in the English translation of this passage which are important here. The verse says: 'But Jesus often withdrew to lonely places and prayed' (Luke 5:16) – though sometimes a translation will use the word 'quiet' rather than 'lonely'. The first important word is 'often', which doesn't appear in the original Greek, yet its inclusion in translation suggests that it is implied. If others were going to say of you, 'This is something they do often', then it would be something which you are regularly doing. 'Often' isn't a word used to suggest occasional involvement, but regular practice. In the Complete Jewish Bible this verse is translated as: 'However, he made a practice of withdrawing to remote places in order to pray.'

Jesus made a regular practice of withdrawing into quiet places for quiet prayer.

And this is the second important word: 'withdrew'. This *is* in the original Greek, and it is a compound word – a word made up of two words placed together, like 'carpark'. The word in Greek is *eimi-hypochoreo*. We will look at the second part first – *hypochoreo*. This word means 'to take a retreat' or 'to retreat away'. The inclusion of this word tells us that this wasn't just Jesus slipping away for a few moments to catch his breath, but that it was a deliberate action of removing himself from the normal everyday life in which he was engaged and taking time out: deliberate, intentional time away from the expectations of life and others. *Eimi* means to just 'be'. No agenda, no plan, no ideas set, just being. Interestingly, *Eimi* is also one of the ways in which the early church is described as gathering together – just 'being' (see Acts 5:12). Perhaps we need to do more gathering as modern church to just 'be' together: no agenda, no plan, no ideas set – just being.

So in this passage of Jesus and the crowds, what we learn from Jesus is a lesson in having a good work–life balance. He regularly practised creating time in his diary to step out of his everyday life and job expectations to go to lonely, solitary, quiet places on retreat, just to 'be' for a while in the Divine presence in prayer – probably quiet or silent prayer, what we might call contemplative prayer. We will expand on what contemplative prayer means in a later chapter, but for now let's draw on another verse of scripture – 'Whoever says that he lives in God must live as Jesus lived' (1 John 2:6, NCV).

Do you say that you live in God? Perhaps you might use the phrase 'Christian' or something similar, rather than 'live in God', but it means the same thing. Do you say you are a Christian? A follower of Christ? Then you should live as Jesus lived. There is so much that we need to learn of how to live from how Jesus lived, but for now, just hold the words from this verse from 1 John in mind and go back and reread this chapter so far again.

So, now you have done that, I have something to say to you. For the first time in this book, but definitely not the last, I am going to make this suggestion:

Stop reading, put the book down, and go and be.

Go and *eimi-hyperchoreo* (which is probably terrible Greek grammar!). Reading about this way of life is helpful and can teach us all sorts of amazing information, knowledge and maybe even wisdom, but, as I said in the introduction, only practice will give you the experiential understanding and conscious awareness which will transform your inner being. As Thomas Merton says about this practice: 'It is a more profound depth of faith, a knowledge too deep to be grasped in images, in words, or even in clear concepts… [It] is always beyond our own knowledge, beyond our own light, beyond systems, beyond explanations, beyond discourse, beyond dialogue, beyond our own self.'[3] It is only comprehendible and comprehensible, if it is ever that at all, through practice and actual interaction with the Divine.

So stop reading, put the book down, and go and be still for a time.

Welcome back!

I don't know how easy you found that: putting down what you were doing and going and just being. There are plenty of books, apps and websites which can help you in how to engage with that effectively.[4] The reality is that you had already set aside time out of your usual routine and daily expectations to read, so perhaps it wasn't so difficult to set the book down and just be. But how do you begin to incorporate this practice into your everyday life? How do you transform your mindset to follow the precedent set by Jesus for the right work–life balance? Our lives are busy, busy, busy! There is so much to do and so little time! Well, at least, that is what we have allowed ourselves to believe. Actually, we always make time for what we believe is important. It just depends upon what you think is important.

One of the responses I often give when someone says to me, 'I don't have time to meditate, or sit and just be,' is that I bet they regularly make time for their physical being, so why do they think they don't need to make time for their inner being? We always make time for what we deem important.

I bet every one of you reading this took time out in the past 48 hours to sleep. Perhaps you might be someone who doesn't think they have the time to regularly practise being still, yet slept for a number of hours in one go within the past 24 or 48 hours. So you had time for your physical being. Why treat your inner being so much worse than your physical being? It needs the same care and attention. It gets exhausted and burned out just like your body. So make time for it as well.

It has been my experience that, as I have made time for my inner being to be still, I have been more effective in the work which I do and I have needed less sleep than I previously needed. But it begins with a change of mindset, a change of belief to one which goes against the mainstream western work ethic.

We need to believe in the benefit of doing nothing.

We need to believe that resting is as important as working.

We need to believe that doing nothing is not wasting time, but a beneficial activity to our own well-being, inner health and growth.

We need to slow down and breath.

We need to live in the Christlike work–life balance.

In my book *The Mystic Path of Meditation* (Anamchara Books, 2013), I give five examples of how we might engage with this mindset of slowing down.[5] These five ways, of expanding time periods, help us live a life centred on this way of being. In the foreword to the book, Ray Simpson suggests everyone should have these five examples displayed on their kitchen or bedroom wall.[6]

The first is to *Meditate Momentarily*. Life offers us small moments scattered throughout our day which we can use to take a few breaths and recentre. Stopped at a traffic light, standing in a queue, travelling in a lift – those sorts of tiny moments.

The next is to *Divert Daily*, to create a small period of time to just sit and be. This is not long, just a few minutes, maybe up to 20 or so when you have practised for a while, but an intentional period of time each day set aside to just be.

Then I suggest we should *Withdraw Weekly*. This is a longer period of time, once a week, maybe up to half a day, to have nothing in your diary. Or, perhaps more accurately, to have 'you' in your diary.

Expanding the amount of time we engage in this important act, I go on to suggest that we should *Make a Date Monthly*. Once a month go away somewhere, to a retreat centre for a day, or to a place we know we can get away from everything, and just go to be and dwell in the Divine presence for a whole day. I know plenty of people who do this to follow the football team that they love, so why shouldn't we do it for the purpose of gaining a deeper relationship with the Divine?

Finally, I suggest we should *Abdicate Annually*. Once a year we should book in a few days to go away on a retreat, an organised one or a personal one. The aim is not to be a tourist, but to soak in, over a few days, the Divine presence, to go away with the express purpose of becoming saturated with the Divine and being still for longer.

Retreats are something which we can all benefit from, but so few people actually engage with them. The quotation with which I started this chapter comes from a talk given by Evelyn Underhill, a wonderful teacher of contemplation and Christian mysticism, at the 1932 annual meeting of the Association for Promoting Retreats. In the same talk she also said:

> Most of us are bitterly conscious of the extent in which we are at the mercy of our surroundings which grow ever more and more insistent in their pressure, their demands on our attention and time; less and less suggestive of Reality, of God. They call out… often with the very best intentions, under the plea of good works, family duties, social obligations, we capitulate to the surface activities of existence, the ceaseless chain of passing events. We forget that awestruck upward glance which is the mark of the spiritual man. Then we lose all sense of proportion, become fussy, restless, full of things that simply must be done, quite oblivious to the only reason anything should be done… We can't rest in the Lord; there really isn't time for that… So we gradually forget what interior silence is like, and seldom enter the interior world… When we have reached this stage, nothing is going to save us but that 'Spot of Re-birth' [which is what a retreat is].[7]

Here Underhill reminds us that the retreat, to go away and spend time intentionally practising the 'awestruck upward glance which is the mark of the spiritual [person]', is essential, and, as she said in the quote at the start of the chapter, going on retreat should be 'part of our normal spiritual routine [where it] will yield on the whole its fullest results when we regard it more often and more generally, in Abbot Delattes's beautiful phrase, as an opportunity of "steeping our souls in the beauty of the mysterious"'. If you have never been on a spiritual retreat, an organised one with teaching input or a personal one on your own, then I would strongly suggest that you go and get your diary now and create a space in it to go away for a few days and be on retreat.[8]

An expansion of the retreat is the spiritual pilgrimage – the intentional journey to a place which is spiritually significant: a sacred space or a thin place, that is, a place where the separation between the natural and the supernatural feels thin.

On a retreat, the destination and what one does there is the focus, but on a pilgrimage, the journey itself is as important as the destination. Pilgrims set aside days, perhaps even weeks or months, to walk a journey which has been walked over centuries by thousands, more likely millions, of people.

The spiritual pilgrimage is the practice of slowing down our physical self to enable our inner self to slow down. To walk intentionally, mindfully, with a conscious awareness of the Divine presence lingering on the road or path from all those previous sacred walkers who came before us.

There are many sacred places around the world where you can engage in pilgrimage. The important thing is to go somewhere which has deep spiritual significance to your own spiritual journey. You are not being a tourist, so don't just type into an online search engine 'where to go on pilgrimage' like you might type in where to go on holiday. Rather, find a place which resonates with your soul, which you will feel a connection to and with as you both walk and arrive.[9]

Undertaking pilgrimage was a popular practice in the Middle Ages in Britain, Ireland and across mainland Europe. At this period of history, many people travelled to spiritually significant places, taking the trip of a lifetime on pilgrimage. However, many of the people who lived then and wanted to go on such a pilgrimage either couldn't afford to leave their homes and livelihoods for such a long period of time or just couldn't afford the cost of the journey.

Over this period a practice became popular to help those who had a desire to go on pilgrimage but couldn't – the practice of walking a labyrinth. You will find in many Medieval cathedrals, and some churches and monastic centres, either tiled into the floor or created outside, a weaving pathway in a circular shape. This is a labyrinth. Unlike a maze or the labyrinth of Greek mythology, these labyrinths have no dead ends, but are one single unhindered path which flows around, back and forth, into the centre. Once at the centre, you then walk the same path back outwards to where you entered.[10] Labyrinths are an ancient pattern and practice, being evidenced to the BCE period, and are still practised by many today.

When walking a labyrinth, one should slow down the pace of each step. This in turn slows the pace of the mind. Walk mindfully and intentionally, perhaps with a specific contemplation in mind. You may even wish to carry an object to represent something which you wish to leave in the Divine hands and presence.

When you reach the centre, pause for as long as you wish. If you are carrying something, put it down, leave it in the centre, releasing it in your inner being and mind into the Divine. Walk slowly away, retracing your steps along the flowing path of the labyrinth until you reach the place where you started. Before you exit the path, pause, lift your head in recognition of the Divine presence, and take the gentle pace of your labyrinth walk with you into the rest of your day.

If you have the privilege to walk a labyrinth with others, note how sometimes you are walking alongside someone, yet on a totally different part of the path, then you will part company, as their path leads them in a different direction. Note too that you may pass someone who is on the way out when you are on the way in, on the same path, but walking in a different direction.

All these things can be a good spiritual metaphor for our life journey.

The practice of walking a labyrinth is a powerful thing.

You can create your own simple labyrinth with the pattern on the following page. I have done this with groups, creating the labyrinth with either pitch-marking spray on grass, stones on a beach or branches and sticks in the woods. The communal act of gathering the stones and wood as a group was a wonderful part of the process.

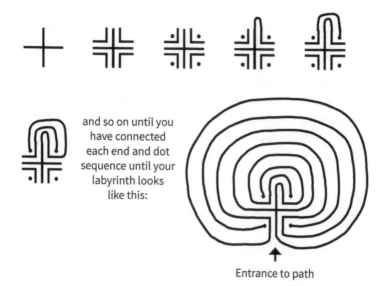

and so on until you have connected each end and dot sequence until your labyrinth looks like this:

Entrance to path

How to create a simple labyrinth

So here we have the first step in our journey of stillness, silence, solitude and sanctuary: the first step, even, in the stillness. That is, we intentionally slow down, or even stop. We make a conscious decision that you will gain the work, life and prayer balance which was exemplified in the story of Jesus near the start of this chapter. We intentionally become still. We create opportunities, from tiny moments in each day to taking a long pilgrimage, to engage with stillness. We intentionally do nothing, which is very different from simply finding yourself with nothing to do. We intentionally slow down, stop, be still.

2

Be still and know

The Lord answered all the questions and doubts that I could raise. Very comfortingly he said to me, 'I may make all things well, I can make all things well, I will make all things well, and I shall make all things well. You will see for yourself that all manner of things will be well.'

Mother Julian of Norwich[1]

I spend a lot of my time travelling around the UK, and often to other countries, teaching retreats and therefore visiting numerous retreat centres. Inevitably one particular verse will be displayed somewhere in some form or translation of the Bible. It is, probably, the most often quoted Bible verse, or at least verse from the Psalms, among contemplatives and those teaching the art of stillness and silence. I am speaking of Psalm 46:10, which begins: 'Be still, and know that I am God.' Different translations begin this verse in different ways, as is the nature of differing translations. I love the collection of words from The Passion Translation, with an extra word in square brackets which the translation footnotes as the word used in the Septuagint:

Surrender your anxiety! [Relax!]
Be silent and realize that I am God.
I am the God above all the nations,

and I am exalted throughout the whole earth.

PSALM 46:10 (TPT)

I find that the superfluous use of words of this translation resonates with me. Instead of just the traditional 'Be still', it flows around, mulls around the idea, the whole concept of the reality of what we are being called to do: 'Surrender your anxiety! [Relax!] Be silent.' By the end of the list, if you really engage with the words, mind, body and soul, you can start to feel more relaxed before you have even got anywhere into the verse, either by simply reading it or by using it as a mantra[2] to repeat and focus your thoughts.

One of the great ways to use this verse is to practise it as a contraction meditation, that is, repeating a sentence or short verse, and then taking away a word or two at a time to help centre and focus your mind and meditation. You can sit and listen to me guide you through it audibly on the meditation app Insight Timer,[3] or you can simply read it here with this simpler, more traditional rendering of words from the first part of the verse.

Sit still and comfortably. Breathe gently and slowly. Follow the words in a way which means that as you use less words, you begin to feel a greater draw towards the centre of your being, and begin to become aware of that centre becoming calm. Repeat each line three times slowly, then sit in silence for a short time after you have reached the final line, as if for the final contraction you are reading the pause which comes before the first word:

Be still and know I am God.
Be still and know I am.
Be still and know.
Be still.
Be.

But this verse, as with all sacred scriptures, is more than just a nice form of relaxing meditation. It is more than just some words to gloss over as you read a chunk of the Bible. They are words which need to seep into our very being and transform our conscious awareness of reality. They need to become part of what forms who we are. Let us go back to The Passion Translation and begin to sit with the words for a while, to really contemplate their meaning in a deeper sense:

Surrender your anxiety! [Relax!]
Be silent and realize that I am God.

To start with, just linger on the words. This is a life instruction. This is the way in which we are to 'be' in the flow of the busy day and the troubles and the loud, brash parts of our existence. We are called to live in a constant conscious awareness of the reality which these words express.

Surrender your anxiety! [Relax!]
Be silent and realize that I am God.

It is very easy, with this translation, to see a parallel with a verse from the New Testament in which we are also instructed to not be anxious about anything – Philippians 4:6–7. Staying with The Passion Translation, this instruction from the apostle Paul says:

Don't be pulled in different directions or worried about a thing. Be saturated in prayer throughout each day, offering your faith-filled requests before God with overflowing gratitude. Tell him every detail of your life, then God's wonderful peace that transcends human understanding, will guard your heart and mind through Jesus Christ.

PHILIPPIANS 4:6–7 (TPT)

Just for a moment, just for contemplative purposes, not for rewriting scripture to bend it to our will, but just to help us focus on this concept of surrender to the Divine to be able to receive Divine peace a little bit more deeply for a moment longer, let us put the words of these verses together and read them as one statement:

> Surrender your anxiety! [Relax!] Be silent and realize that I am God… Don't be pulled in different directions or worried about a thing. Be saturated in prayer throughout each day, offering your faith-filled requests before God with overflowing gratitude. Tell him every detail of your life, then God's wonderful peace that transcends human understanding, will guard your heart and mind through Jesus Christ.

What an incredible statement!

May I suggest that once again you stop reading, put the book down, and go and be still for a time with these words, or at least the reality of this concept, percolating in your inner being.

Welcome back once again.

Now that we have allowed those words, in their richness and depth, to seep into our being, how do we actually put them into practice? 'It's a nice idea,' you might be thinking, 'to surrender my anxiety; to relax; to be silent and stop my inner striving; to not be pulled in different directions or worried about a thing, but that just seems a million miles away from the reality in which I live. Have you seen what I have to do in a day or deal with in life?'

It is no accident that chapter 2 in this book follows chapter 1. I didn't write a collection of separate thoughts down and then just throw them together. There is a process to go through, a path to follow, a way to walk. Like all aspects of nature, one thing leads to another. As the old adage says, we must learn to walk before we can run. This isn't to restrict us in our movements, it is simply the reality of development.

So it is with the progression along the contemplative path: a process of one thing into another. The first chapter was about slowing down; this chapter is about being still. You have to slow down before you can be still. Think of a runner crossing the finish line and coming to a state of rest to catch their breath. That's the natural process. But there is a transcendent depth to the particular 'being still' which we are talking about here. There is the realisation within this stillness that the Divine presence saturates all things and all aspects of our being. It is in this stillness that we will 'know I am God' and that 'the peace of God, which transcends all understanding, will guard your hearts and minds'. There is a sense of letting go and releasing control of our 'self' and becoming more through trust in the Divine. We will, as the apostle Paul also said, 'be transformed by the renewing of [our] mind' (Romans 12:2).

This transformation has a direct input–output ratio. The level of our input relates directly to the level of output. However, notice that it says 'be transformed' and not 'transform yourselves'. This is a Divine work within us, not something we do. So what is our part in this transformation? It is simple: it is to let go and let God (another statement I frequently see on posters and pictures in retreat centres). We need to release control of our ego and allow the Divine transformation to happen without hindering it or thinking we know better.

The natural process of this begins to transform who we are, to transform the very essence of our being, from what some mystics and spiritual teachers call the false self into our true self.

One such person is Thomas Merton, who tells us that 'every one of us is shadowed by an illusory person: a false self' and that we clothe this false self with our thirst for pleasures, experiences, power, honour, knowledge and love. We 'clothe this false self and construct its nothingness into something objectively real'.[4] This false self, however, according to Merton, is hollow and empty. He describes it in a way which reminds me of the story of *The Invisible Man* by H.G. Wells. Merton says:

> I wind experiences around myself and cover myself with pleasures and glory like bandages in order to make myself perceptible to myself and to the world, as if I were an invisible body that could only become visible when something visible covered its surface. But there is no substance under the things with which I am clothed. I am hollow… and when they are gone there will be nothing left of me but my own nakedness and emptiness and hollowness, to tell me that I am my own mistake.[5]

Merton says that 'all sin starts from the assumption that my false self, the self that exists only in my own egocentric desires, is the fundamental reality of life to which everything else in the universe is ordered'.[6] Merton then goes on in the same and following chapter to talk about the life driven by sin, which is 'a life devoted to the cult of this shadow [self]'.[7] However, in the transforming process of the Divine within us, we begin the journey to the true self, the self which was Divinely created and is the very essence, or image, of God within us. 'At that moment,' Merton says, 'the point of our contact with Him opens out and we pass through the centre of our own nothingness and enter into infinite reality, where we awaken as our true self.'[8] We can be still, relax, stop striving and know that the Divine is God, and that all things will be well.

The quote with which I started this chapter might be familiar to you. It is a quote from the *Revelations of Divine Love* by Mother Julian of Norwich. The more familiar quotation you might know is: 'All shall be well, and all shall be well, and all manner of thing shall be well.' This quotation, both in its more familiar form as well as how it appears at the beginning of this chapter, and other wording can be found in Julian's Thirteenth Revelation. This Revelation is her wondering about the origins of sin, and what would have been if God had not let it happen. The response to her from Jesus, who is the one giving her these revelations of Divine love, is that sin is in the world and it causes pain, but all will be well. She goes on to say:

> On one occasion our good Lord said, 'All things will be well', on another, 'You will see for yourself that all manner of things will be well.' In both these statements we can see different levels of meaning. One was this: that Christ wants us to know that he takes care not only of the noble and great things but also of the humble and small, lowly and simple things – all are equal. That is what he means by 'All manner of things will be well'. He wants us to know that the least thing will not be forgotten.[9]

We can be assured that even the smallest aspect of our lives and our selves will be well, that the Divine has all things in hand, that we can be still and know that the Divine is God, right down to the smallest aspect of life.

This was no empty concept to Mother Julian. She wasn't someone who lived a sheltered life closed away in some palace, or a closeted life in a nice spiritual bubble. The world around her was in a terrible state, covered in the plague and much other destitution. She was most likely a Beguine and became an anchorite – being walled up in a small dwelling, never to be outside again, with only four openings: one to the world outside, so that she could give spiritual direction; one into the church, which she had been walled up against, so that she could join in with the services and partake in the Mass; one where her food and water would come in; and one where the waste of those things would go out. Yet despite Mother Julian going through all that she went through, she discovered a close intimate connection with the Divine. In her book *The Beguines*, Silvana Panciera states that 'the discovery of such a familiar God predisposes us to trusting and joy, sentiments of which [Mother Julian's] book is full'.[10]

Discovering such a close relationship with the Divine, and being transformed from our false selves into our true selves, brings us to a place where we can be still and know and trust that the Divine is God and that all will be well; it predisposes us to trusting.

You may well say again, 'That's a nice idea, but have you seen what I have to do in a day or deal with in life?' But we have examples from many in our spiritual heritage who did just that in the midst of all they were going through. We will meet others as we continue to travel through this book.

We have slowed down and become still and gained a sense of our true selves, but we need to be able to maintain this practice within the everyday aspects of our lives. We need to be able to live centred lives in the midst of all we have to do, and not just in the moments when we can step out and find space. We need to be still here and now, to be fully present in the eternal now.

3

Still here

He was never hasty nor loitering, but did each thing in its season, with an even, uninterrupted composure and tranquillity of spirit. 'The time of business,' said he, 'does not with me differ from the time of prayer; and in the noise and clatter of my kitchen, while several persons are at the same time calling for different things [of me], I possess God in as great a tranquillity as if I were upon my knees at the blessed sacrament.'

M. Beaufort, describing Brother Lawrence[1]

We are in the midst of a growing interest in mindfulness in our modern western culture. Mindfulness courses and retreats, books, websites, social media pages and apps abound, some good, some not so good. If you type the word 'mindfulness' into an internet search engine, you get over 22 million results! The mindfulness entry on Wikipedia says, 'Mindfulness is the psychological process of purposely bringing one's attention to experiences occurring in the present moment without judgment, which one develops through the practice of meditation and through other training.'[2]

This webpage also states that mindfulness comes from the Buddhist tradition, and references a particular teacher from that tradition called Thich Nhat Hanh. In his book *The Miracle of Mindfulness*, Hanh states:

Mindfulness is at the same time a means and an end, the seed and the fruit. When we practise mindfulness in order to build up concentration, mindfulness is the seed. But mindfulness itself is the life of awareness: the presence of mindfulness means the presence of life, and therefore mindfulness is also the fruit. Mindfulness frees us from forgetfulness and dispersion and makes it possible to live fully each minute of life. Mindfulness enables us to live.[3]

However, despite the claim from Wikipedia and the connection of mindfulness in many people's minds with Buddhism, the truth is that this practice is deeply rooted in the Christian tradition and can be found in many great names from the Christian heritage. We will discover some of them and what they have to say about this practice as we progress through this chapter, but first I want to throw out some conjectures as to why in recent years there has been, and continues to be, an interest in the west in this practice, especially from those who may view themselves as 'not religious' or 'non-spiritual'.

Over the past few decades, there has been an increase of activity and busy-ness in our western culture, a growth in the expectation of productivity. This has happened simultaneously with a gradual increase in depression and a general plummeting of mental health. In the two decades between the late 1990s and the late 2010s, the dispensing of antidepressants in the UK rose from around 15 million to over 40 million. Almost 50% of this increase happened in the years immediately following the 2008 global financial crisis, which was the catalyst of the global Great Recession. The general mental health of an entire nation fell because of the financial situation and the pressure people felt about life.

That increase in pressure, along with a growing understanding of mental health over the past few decades, has brought about the desire by many to try to balance out their lives without, or alongside, medication.

If you have been prescribed antidepressant medication, then always follow your doctor's advice. But alongside this, and for those who are perhaps struggling with fluctuating or low mental health who are not on medication, meditation, especially mindfulness meditation, can be a great help. I have known GPs to prescribe, along with anti-anxiety and antidepressant medication, mindfulness courses.

The practices of becoming fully present in the present moment and of focused awareness are incredibly beneficial for bringing a balance to one's mental health.

The basics are this: we have three aspects to our being – the physical, the mental and the emotional (we will come back to the spiritual later; this is a description for those who view themselves as 'not religious' or 'non-spiritual'). You might term these three aspects as body, mind and soul.

The practice of mindfulness is to become fully present in the present moment: to be here now, to be still here, now. It is to practise aligning these three aspects of ourselves to be focused in and on the present moment. It can be explained something like this:

Our body is always fully present in the present moment. We can only be physically present in one place at a time. As helpful as it would be to be able to be physically present in more than one place at a time, that is just not possible. We are always physically fully present in the present moment. However, most of the time our mind is not present in the present moment. It is off somewhere in the future or in the past. It is thinking about something which has happened or which will or might happen. Whether that thing is only moments away or further off in time, our mind is usually not fully present in the present moment. It wanders. It drifts off. It is thinking of something which is not the something which is happening in the present moment. Naturally, when our mind thinks of something, we have an emotional reaction. We feel happy or sad; we feel joyful or anxious. It is a natural process that our emotional self – our soul, for the purpose of this explanation – follows the mind and responds to it.

If this is the case – that our mind is almost never in the present moment but off somewhere in the past or future, and our soul naturally follows it there – then that means that for most of your life, two-thirds of you is not even present in the present moment in which you are living. It is just your body, and that is only there because it cannot be anywhere else. The practice of mindfulness is to train our minds to be present in the present moment. If we train our cognitive self, our mind, to be fully present in the present moment, then our soul follows it. Therefore we will have all three aspects of ourselves present. We will be fully present in the present moment: a phrase used regularly among mindfulness teachers.

The present moment is, for us as we are within the flow of time, the only moment that exists. As Master Oogway says in *Kung Fu Panda*, 'Yesterday is history, tomorrow is a mystery, but today is a gift. That is why it is called the present.'[4] This gift of the present moment is lost on most of us because we are not aware of it. This moment is, by the contemplatives and mystics, known as the Eternal Now. The Eternal Now is the moment we are in in this actual moment. The moment you were in when you began to read this paragraph has gone; you read the quotation by Master Oogway in the past, but this moment, the moment which exists as you read this word, is the Eternal Now, the only moment which exists. The past 'now' has passed; it is gone. Only the now 'now' exists. The Eternal Now is an ever-flowing singular moment, which is fleeting yet eternal.

It is at this point that I want to bring in the spiritual concept of our selves. It is only in the Eternal Now moment that God can speak to us, because it is the only moment in which we exist. So if your mind and soul and spirit are not present in the Eternal Now moment, how will you hear the Divine voice or be aware of the Divine energy prompting you?

Mindfulness meditation is the practice which leads us to the mindful awareness of the present moment each and every moment. Mindfulness meditation trains our cognitive self, our mind, to remain focused and aware in the present moment, and then we are able to hear the Divine voice, feel the Divine movement and fully live a life of awareness.

Living in a mindful state is to live a life in awareness – awareness of yourself, awareness of the world around you and awareness of the Divine presence. One of the Christian teachers who spoke about what we now understand as 'mindfulness', before its explosion of popularity in the last couple of decades, was the Indian Jesuit priest Anthony DeMello. DeMello ran courses and retreats in the mid- to late-20th century, which became books on what he called 'awareness'. Awareness for DeMello was the waking up (enlightenment) of our true selves to the Reality within reality. Awareness was to live with a non-judgemental understanding of everything. Judgement for him was opposite to awareness and understanding. Awareness and understanding are to not label anything, because understanding has stopped the moment you label something. 'No judgement, no commentary, no attitude:

one simply observes, one studies, one watches, without the desire to change [or label] what is. Because if you desire to change what is into what you think *should* be, you no longer understand',[5] and awareness has disappeared. This is mindful awareness: living in the awareness of what is, without imposing your own ideas or agenda upon it, just observing without judgement. Long before any other books came out on Christian mindfulness, DeMello was writing the same thing in different semantics. No book on Christian mindfulness has ever surpassed DeMello's. If you want to read a good modern (late 20th-century) Christian perspective on mindfulness, start with *Awareness* by Anthony DeMello. You may not need to move on.

A traditional way in mindfulness of focusing and living in this aware-ness, especially for beginners, is to use breathing techniques, to focus on the breath flowing in and out of the body to help focus the mind. This might be seen by many as one of those things which is part of the Buddhist practice, but there are instructions within Christian her-itage of using breathing techniques for mindfulness from centuries ago: 'It is not out of place to teach people, especially beginners, that they should... introduce their own mind to themselves through con-trol of breathing,' says St Gregory Palamas, a 14th-century Byzantine theologian and monk of Mount Athos (in modern-day Greece) who became archbishop of Thessaloniki and the defender of Hesychasm. Beginners, he says, will find that their mind wanders after they have tried to focus it. 'This is why,' he says, 'certain masters recommend them to control the movement inwards and outwards of the breath, and to hold it back a little; in this way they will also be able to control the mind together with the breath... recollection [focused mindful awareness] is a spontaneous effect of the attention of the mind, for the to-and-fro movement of the breath becomes quieted during intensive reflection [on it] especially with those who maintain inner quiet in body and soul.'[6]

By this practice of controlled breathing we can live in mindful awareness.

But how does this living in mindful awareness enable us to better connect with the Divine presence surrounding us and saturating our entire being?

Well, first it causes us to be fully present in the present moment, which is, as we have already discovered, the only moment which exists and therefore the only moment in which we are able to hear the Divine voice or feel the Divine move. But, more than this, it enables us to get on with our normal, everyday activities without losing that sense of the Divine presence.

The quotation with which I began this chapter comes from the teachings of and about Nicholas Herman of Lorraine, who, when admitted as a lay brother into the discalced Parisian Carmelites in 1666, became known as Brother Lawrence. The teachings come as transcribed conversations and letters collectively today known as *The Practice of the Presence of God*. In essence, this is Christian mindfulness at its best, found in a 17th-century Parisian monastery taught by the monastery baker, a 'lowly and unlearned man'.[7]

In this incredible little book, Brother Lawrence explains how he had come to the ability to live in the constant awareness of the Divine presence in all that he did, in the busy work hours as much as the quiet hours set for prayer. His process was that he used the hours of prayer appointed by the monastery to 'convince his mind of, and to impress deeply upon his heart, the Divine existence… [and] by this short and sure method he exercised himself in the knowledge and love of God, resolving to use his upmost endeavour to live in a continual sense of His Presence'.[8]

Brother Lawrence was the baker of the monastery. And in every small activity he did in the kitchen, he began and ended with the recognition of the Divine presence. By doing these things, by spending time in quiet prayer, saturating himself in the Divine presence and then consciously remaining in the awareness of the Divine throughout everything he did, he had 'come to a state wherein it would be as difficult for me to not think of God as it was at first to accustom myself to it'.[9]

In this statement by Brother Lawrence, we find two encouraging things. First, that it is possible, through mindful practice, to get to a state where we can be continually aware of the Divine presence. Second, that when we first begin this practice, it is a difficult one. Brother Lawrence found it hard to get accustomed to the continual awareness of the Divine, but through dedicated practice, he did. Brother Lawrence says:

> This practice of the Presence of God is somewhat hard at the outset, yet, pursued faithfully, it works imperceptibly within the soul most marvellous effects; it draws down God's grace abundantly, and leads the soul insensibly to the ever-present vision of God, loving and beloved, which is the most spiritual and real, the most free and most life-giving manner of prayer… [so] be not disheartened at your many falls; truly this habit can only be formed with difficulty, yet when it is formed, how great will be your joy therein![10]

Continue to practise; don't give up. A spiritual discipline is not easily formed into a habit. It takes time and effort, but once it is formed into a habit, it begins to form who you are. You begin to be able to live in the continual awareness of the Divine presence.

One of the ways we can form this habit is through another practice within the Christian tradition which helps us to be 'still here', that is, still and focused in the present moment so we can live in the continual awareness of the Divine presence – the practice of Centring Prayer. Although Centring Prayer is not the same as mindfulness, it has an element of drawing one's focus in to become centred in the Eternal Now. To gain a fuller understanding of the beginnings and heart of this practice, I suggest you read *Intimacy with God: An introduction to Centring Prayer* by Thomas Keating. But for the purpose of this book, I want to focus on one aspect of Centring Prayer – the use of the 'sacred word'.

Centring Prayer is largely based upon the 14th-century English monastic text called *The Cloud of Unknowing*. This was written by an unknown author, but is assumed to be the teachings of a senior monk to either young or novice monks in the art of contemplation, especially the art of contemplative living in daily life.

The part of *The Cloud*, as it is often called, from which the sacred word of Centring Prayer comes is found in chapter 37, entitled 'Personal prayers of diligent contemplatives'. It says:

> Contemplatives seldom use words when they pray, but if they do, they choose only a few, and the fewer the better. They prefer a short one-syllable word over two syllables, because the spirit can best assimilate it. This one word keeps the person engaged in this spiritual exercise fit and at the top of their form, so to speak.[11]

I love this contraction of the use of words to exemplify the contemplative life of prayer. The contemplative seldom uses words – most of their prayer life is silent, it is purely mindful awareness of the Divine – but if they *have* to use words they will use as few as possible, and one word would be better than two, and if that one word could just be one syllable, then that is even better! This reflects something from 700 years before *The Cloud*, when John Climacus, in *The Ladder of Divine Ascent*, in which he sets out 30 steps to Theosis or Union with the Divine, says, 'Do not attempt to talk much when you pray lest your mind be distracted in searching for words... Loquacity in prayer often distracts the mind and leads to phantasy, whereas monologia [repetition of a single word or sentence] makes for concentration.'[12] Why is this the case? *The Cloud* goes on to explain that when a person wishes to get a deep and intense message across, one of great importance, a single word with full intent of the heart is sufficient. *The Cloud* uses the example of someone caught in a building on fire. They do not lean out of the window and give an eloquent speech about fire and how the building is burning around them, and how wonderful it would be if someone would possibly help them out, thank you very much. No, in this situation:

> There's no time for babbling or big words – you'll scream, 'FIRE!' or 'HELP!' and this one-word outburst works best... The same is true spiritually. When a little word of one syllable is not just thought or spoken but is an expression of the deepest intentions of your spirit, it is the height of contemplation. (For the spirit height and depth, length and breadth are all one place.) This simple prayer gets God's attention more quickly than any long Psalm mumbled mindlessly through closed teeth. That's why the Scriptures say 'a short prayer penetrates heaven'... Why does this little prayer of one small syllable penetrate heaven? Because you pray it with all that you are and all that you can be.[13]

The scripture reference is to Jesus' first teaching to his disciples on prayer in Matthew 6, where he tells his disciples that the heart of prayer is to find a quiet space and use few words (Matthew 6:5–7).

The examples given in *The Cloud* of single-syllable words to use are 'Love' and 'God'. These words help you focus intently and enable you to penetrate heaven. If you keep a single word as a focus throughout the day, then this awareness goes with you throughout the day, in all you do, through that one single sacred word.

Centring Prayer takes this idea of a single word used and suggests that it can be the way to bring your focus back in line when you find your mind has wandered.

The use of the sacred word enables us to become and remain more centred and aware of the Divine presence in the present moment. Once you have become centred again, the sacred word can be allowed to drift off and we remain in the focused silence of the present moment. Our conscious awareness moves from the surface awareness of the everyday to something much deeper. As Keating says:

> Our consciousness can be likened to a river, with our thoughts passing like boats along its surface. The surface of the river represents our ordinary psychological level of awareness. But a river also has its depths, and so does our awareness. Beneath the ordinary psychological level of awareness, there is a spiritual level of awareness where our intellect and will are functioning in their own proper way in a spiritual manner. Deeper still, or more 'centred', is the Divine Indwelling where the divine energy is present as the source of our being and inspiration at every moment. Personal effort and grace meet at the most centred or inward part of our being, which the mystics call the 'ground of being'.[14]

Gaining and living in this deeper level of conscious awareness, connected to the Divine presence which dwells at the very centre of our being, is the practice of the presence of God which Brother Lawrence spoke of. It is the life of the contemplative which the author of *The Cloud* spoke of; it is the recollection of the mind that Gregory Palamas spoke of; it is the awakened awareness which Anthony DeMello spoke of; and it is the constant conscious awareness of the Divine presence which mindfulness practice leads us to.

Through this practice, through this life, we are able to be still in the present moment, to be still, here and now, whatever the outward expressions of life look like in each moment. We live a life in inner stillness, undisturbed by the outer experiences. One of the other things about plumbing the depths of the river is that when the storms of life come and greatly disturb the surface level of conscious awareness, when the storms rock the boats that are our thoughts, when the raging winds stir up rough waves – what we discover is the deeper we are dwelling in the water, the less these things affect us. The wind and storm only affect the surface of the water; they do not affect the depths. The more deeply we are grounded and centred, the less the storms will affect us. They still happen, but as we practise this mindful awareness, we become more acutely aware of the Divine at the centre, and so we are more able to remain still and unperturbed. This deep level of inner stillness draws us into deep silence.

A mindfulness practice

Stop where you are.

Breathe.

Slow your breathing down a little.

Breathe more deeply.

Become aware of your breath flowing in and out of your body.

Become aware of the sounds around you.

Don't judge them, don't work out what they are, just become aware of them.

Look around you.

Become aware of all that there is around you to see.

No judgement – just awareness of what is.

Are there any aromas flowing through the air you are breathing?

Again, just become aware of them, no judgement of 'nice' or 'nasty'. Don't try to work out what the aromas are, just become aware of them.

As you sit and become fully aware of the physical world around you, remind yourself that the Divine is present here, now, in this Eternal Now moment. The Divine is there with you.

Focus your mind on this.

Allow your inner being the freedom to become aware of the Divine presence.

Just sit in this mindful awareness for a while.

When you get up from this place to continue with the day, take this awareness with you, and live in the awareness and peace.

Part II

Silence

4

In pursuit of silence

> To seek an experience of silence is futile, because to do so is to
> seek an interpretation you have already made; you are running
> after a projection of a virtual artifact already fixed in the mind.
> It is a circular exercise that locks the person deeper into a fan-
> tasy world of his or her own creation: either the expectation
> will never be met, or else one will end in a solipsistic prison of
> stereotypes, which are ultimately unsatisfactory.
>
> Maggie Ross[1]

We live in a world of constant audible distraction, some of which is
thrust upon us and some of which we inflict upon ourselves. There
is nothing wrong, in itself, with having sound around us, especially if
we choose to have it. As I write this, in fact, I have soft instrumental
music playing in the background. But we do need to ensure that we
also switch it off on regular occasions. In the same way that we need
to follow the example of Christ in regularly creating the time to get
away, we need to follow his example of finding *quiet* places to go to.

This might not sound very appealing to you. You might think that finding quiet or silent space is something you don't want to do. We have, in
fact, been conditioned in our society to perceive silence as something
negative. We see it as being restrained from the ability to give our

opinion or our side of the story. Perhaps when we were children we were told to be quiet and stop talking when we felt we had something important to say or add to a discussion. Or we may have been given silence as a punishment, and were made to sit in silence as a consequence of doing something wrong. Perhaps as adults we have been told that no one cares or wants to know our opinion or what we think, so we should stay silent. Or perhaps we have experienced the 'stony silence' of those we once thought friends but who are now ignoring us over some disagreement or falling out.

We have been conditioned to perceive silence as a restraint from expressing ourselves. But this is not all silence is. As human beings, we are very good at focusing on the negative aspect of things. We choose to ignore or fail to see that, if there is a negative side to something, there must, by definition, also be a positive. We shall look at this later in this chapter when we visit a 19th-century Russian Orthodox monk known for silence.

But for now, know that silence can be positive; it can, in fact, be life-giving!

The trouble is that positive silence is elusive and illusory. Like trying to catch a slippery eel, just when we feel we might have achieved silence, it slips away from us. Or, at least, that might be how it seems. But perhaps it is just that you have been looking for the wrong thing. In the quote at the start of this chapter, from the book *Silence: A user's guide* (although it is more like an academic study – 'user guides' are usually a bit more accessible and easy to understand), Maggie Ross, an English Anglican solitary, tells us that when we seek an experience of silence, what we are really seeking is our own perception of what silence is. This is a futile act, as usually our perception is fantasy. She goes on to say, however, that the silence which the mystics found and speak of is the silence which is beyond the egotistic perception of what silence should be; it was something much deeper, something which connects our own consciousness with the deeper, more transcendent Divine mind dwelling within us. She says:

> The work of silence restores free exchange and mutual inter-dependence between the two ways of knowing – between the self-conscious mind and the deep mind… the work of silence effects a shift that re-centres the source from which the person draws energy, from the self-conscious mind to the deep mind. One of the consequences of this shift is that the person realises that this 'centre' is everywhere, and that what once had been perceived as boundaries are nowhere.[2]

This shift in realisation enables us to encounter this deeper silence everywhere and be freed from all boundaries which might have previously restrained us. Silence changes from something elusive to something attainable, because we are free from our expectations, preconceived ideas and fantasy versions of silence.

The reality is that silence, understood as a lack or absence of all sound, is, in fact, a fantasy: we cannot be totally free from sound. This version of silence does not exist. There will always be sound around us. For a wonderful and interesting look at this, at our relationship with sound and silence, watch the documentary film from which this chapter title comes.[3] Here are some insights from the documentary:

> [One might ask] does [silence] exist in a decibel sense? A noise sense, or a lack of noise sense? And the literature is clear that silence doesn't exist in that sense. (7m30s)

When we throw around the term of silence, we may in the first instance imagine that we are seeking some kind of absolute quiet… What we are looking for, I came to believe, is more a kind of balance in our environment. It's the particular balance of sound and quiet which maximises our perceptual awareness of where we are. (31m00s)

Silence is where we hear something deeper than our chatter, and silence is where we speak something deeper than our words. All of us know that the most essential things in life are exactly what we can't express. Our relation to faith, our relation to love, our relation to death, our relation to divinity. So I think silence is the resting place of everything essential. (23m35s)

If we start to cultivate an appreciation of silence as the precious thing it is, and enjoy it for a few minutes a day, then it gives us a proper relationship with sound, with noise, with our own sound. It allows us to be much more balanced in the way that we relate to the world, much more conscious. (30m39s)

When does [a sound] become 'noise'?… [It is when we say] this particular sound is intruding on what I am trying to do. This is unwanted, unpleasant sound. (46m37s)

I want to take this final quote from the film and expand on it a little, because this may help us in our pursuit of silence.

It is clear that, as with the first quotation from the film, silence in the sense of 'lack of noise' does not exist. So how do we find a sense of the silent? I believe that the final quotation here from the film holds part of the answer, if we mix it with a little of our mindfulness understanding from the previous chapter.

We learned that mindfulness is a practice of simple awareness, of just being aware or mindful of our environment, internally as well as externally, without judgement. Bringing this idea into the pursuit of silence, if we sit in simple awareness of the sounds around us, making no judgement of what those sounds are or whether we like them or not, then we are able to sit without distraction.

It is not, in fact, the noise itself which we find a distraction, but our judgement and perception of that sound. It becomes a distraction when we decide that it is unpleasant or unwanted.

I shall give you an example. Imagine that you are sitting in a garden which is perfectly peaceful. The only sound you hear is the breeze, softly passing by. This is as close to audible silence as you can get. Then a flock of small birds comes and lands in the tree nearby and start to chirp. You then decide to switch on some calming music. These sounds aid you in your meditation. Why? Because you judge them to be 'nice' and 'helpful'.

Now start this visualisation again. Imagine that you are sitting in a garden which is perfectly peaceful. The only sound you hear is the breeze, softly passing by. Then two children nearby start to argue and one begins to cry. Then someone starts up a lawnmower or grass trimmer. You are now totally distracted! I want you to imagine that the crying and arguing children are at the same volume as the flock of birds which landed in the tree, and the grass-cutting machine is at the same volume as your music was. Why do you find one pleasant and helpful towards your meditation and the other horrible and distracting?

The answer is not because of the volume of the sounds or even what the sounds themselves are; the answer is in your judgement of the sounds. Even if the birds were not your choice, though the music was, you still didn't find them distracting. They may have invaded your 'silence', but you liked it. This judgement of the sounds causes one to be helpful and one to be distracting. If you practise simple awareness of sounds rather than judgement, then nothing is a distraction: no judgement, no distraction. You are then able to meditate wherever you are, no matter what is going on around you. You are able to create an inner environment of silence, of a sense of inner peace which does not get distracted by the external circumstances or sounds. And it is this kind of silence, of inner peace and lack of distraction, that the mystics speak of. And it is here that we meet the 19th-century Russian Orthodox monk I mentioned earlier.

Seraphim of Sarov (sometimes Zarov) was a priest and monk at the turn of the 19th century. He is most famous for moving out of the monastery into a hermitage in the mountains in Sarov, spending 25 years there as a solitary hermit and later spiritual director, with 16 years of that time in solitary silence. Over this time he cultivated an incredible sense of inner peace and Divine tranquillity.

He is famous for saying, 'Acquire the Spirit of Peace and a thousand souls around you will be saved.' Expanding on that, he said:

> There is nothing better than peace in Christ, for it brings victory over all the evil spirits on earth and in the air. When peace dwells in a person's heart, it enables him to contemplate the grace of the Holy Spirit from within. Those who live in peace collect spiritual gifts as it were with a scoop, and shed the light of knowledge on others. All our thoughts, all our desires, all our efforts, and all our actions should make us say constantly… 'O Lord, give us peace!'' When people live in peace, God reveals mysteries to them.

There is a wonderful story I heard of the indwelling peace in Seraphim affecting another. In this story we can see what Seraphim might have meant by thousands being saved through us acquiring the Spirit of Peace. As I mentioned before, we are good at focusing on the negative side of things without realising that that must mean there is a positive alternative. So before I tell you the story of Seraphim, let me give you the negative example, which, I have no doubt, you will be able to relate to.

Imagine you are sitting in a room quietly minding your own business, maybe reading a book or doing something else calming, feeling happy in the peaceful atmosphere. Suddenly someone bursts into the room in a terrible mood and with a foul temper! They bring with them a whirlwind of negative emotions which totally change the atmosphere in the room. They are projecting their negative energy into the room, which then begins to affect you. You begin to feel their negativity; you might even begin to feel what they are projecting. As human beings, we physically run on energy, just like the rest of creation. When we get stressed, we can get a headache; if that stress is prolonged, we can get a stomach ulcer. Stress is an emotional aspect of our being, but the headache and ulcer are physical responses, because we are holistic beings: each aspect of our being – mind, body, soul and spirit – affects the other aspects. So we project the energy which we are feeling. It is just something that happens. That is the negative example, and as we know full well, if there is a negative example, then there is an opposite, positive example. So let me tell you the story from the life of Seraphim.

There was once a young student in Russia who suffered from terrible anxiety. He had head and stomach pains from this anxiety, which affected him entirely. Whatever he tried to calm himself down, whether drugs or meditation, he could not be rid of the deep-seated anxiety which plagued him. It affected him physically, psychologically and spiritually. One day he heard someone speak of a monk in Sarov who had become a starets, an elder in a monastery and one who functions as venerated adviser and teacher. This starets, Seraphim by name, was most famous for being at peace and teaching others how to be at peace. So the student decided that he would go to Sarov and speak to this starets.

Sarov was 400 miles away, but undeterred this student set out, walking for almost three weeks to visit the monastery. When he arrived and the door was opened, he was told that Seraphim was no longer at this monastery. The student's heart sank. But he was reassured, as Seraphim had only moved to a hermitage in the mountains behind the monastery. The student thanked the monk at the door and continued his journey to find Seraphim. Up the mountain the student went, his anxiety no less than ever before. When he reached the hut where he was told Seraphim would be, he knocked on the door. But there was no answer. No one was there.

The student walked around the hut, looking for the monk, but he could not find him anywhere. As the student walked through the vegetable patch at the back of the hut, he noticed a pile of clothes in the corner. As he got closer, he realised that it was not a pile of clothes, but Seraphim curled up asleep in the vegetable patch. The student, out of respect, did not wish to disturb his sleep, and so quietly sat next to the sleeping monk. Seraphim did not wake, but remained asleep for a long time. However, as the student sat and waited for the monk to wake, so he could speak to him and be taught about Divine inner peace, the student felt, for the first time in as long as he could remember, a sense of peace begin to rest gently upon him. Gradually over the time he sat there, all his anxiety drifted away and he began to feel a deep sense of peace and the gentle touch of the Divine upon his heart. With a smile, the student quietly got up, so as not to disturb the monk, and walked back down the mountain, past the monastery and the 400 miles back home, with a deep sense of peace in the core of his being.

This is a wonderful little story which illustrates for us the fact that what we have in the core of our being, in our hearts, naturally flows out from us, even when we are asleep! If the core is in discord, then that is what will flow out from us. But if our core is filled with Divine peace, then *that* is what will flow out from us. As the Quakers say: 'In silence which is active, the Inner Light begins to glow – a tiny spark… It is by an attention full of love that we enable the Inner Light to blaze and illuminate our dwelling and to make of our whole being a source from which this Light may shine out.'[4]

The answer, then, in our pursuit of silence, is to enter the silent land of Divine peace and have it fill our heart, the core of our very being.

Before we move on to the next chapter about going into the silent land, pause for a while and do this simple exercise.

Begin by sitting comfortably, closing your eyes and bringing your breathing down to a slower, deeper rhythm than your usual breathing rhythm.

Become aware of your inner being and what the dominant emotion is within you at this moment. Then bring to mind any anxiety or worry you have. Become aware of how your inner being changes.

Repeat the following words from Philippians 4:6-7:

> Do not be anxious about anything, but in every situation, by prayer and petition, with thanksgiving, present your requests to God. And the peace of God, which transcends all

understanding, will guard your hearts and your minds in Christ Jesus.

Release your anxieties into the Divine presence. Let them go. Visualise yourself doing this. In your mind's eye, see yourself releasing these things in the Divine presence.

Now open your hands and your heart to receive the Divine peace promised once you have released your anxieties into the Divine hands.

Sit for a while feeling and resting in this.

In your own time, slowly open your eyes and become fully present again in the place where you are.

Allow the God of peace (Philippians 4:9) to remain with you as you step into the rest of your day.

5

Into the silent land

We enter the land of silence by the silence of surrender, and there is no map of the silence that is surrender. There are skills, however, by which we learn to dispose ourselves to surrender and thus to discover this uncharted land.

Martin Laird[1]

The words 'surrender' and 'obedience' do not sit well with people in today's western world. For most people, the words provoke resistance, being associated with restrictions to their freedom and life. This may well be true in some cases of physical life, and certainly history has shown this to be true. However, when we are talking about the inner and spiritual journey, the journey into the silent land, then these words are essential.

In the New Monastic community[2] of which I am a vowed member, we commit to the three foundational principles of traditional monasticism, which are poverty, chastity and obedience, although we have adjusted them. As a dispersed community (not a residential community), we do not have a monastic centre, but each member commits to live out our Rule, or Way of Life as we call it, in their own home and community, family and local church. So we have adjusted the basic principles slightly to be more appropriate: poverty has become simplicity, and chastity has become purity. I expand on this more fully in chapter 9. However, we have kept the foundational rule of *obedience*. We didn't feel that this was something that a member of a dispersed New Monastic community couldn't commit to – obedience to the Rule and obedience to God. But what does that actually mean? What does it mean to surrender and live in obedience to the Divine?

To help us unpack this a little, let us look at the roots of these words:

Surrender ('give up control/power'), from Latin *sur* ('up' or 'over') and *render*, from *re* ('back to original') and *do/der* ('to give').

Obedience ('submit to authority'), from Latin *ob* ('towards') and *audire* ('listen' or 'hear').[3]

These root meanings help us to understand better how these acts might fit well with our contemplative journey. We must, as many of the mystics of Christian and other heritages tell us, give up egotistic control of our 'selves' in total surrender to the Divine, and in this surrender we listen deeply to the voice of the Divine, which is silence. God's first language is silence, as the 16th-century Carmelite mystic John of the Cross said. This is what the prophet Elijah experienced when he was up on the mountain. In 1 Kings 19 Elijah goes out on the mountain and is told that the Lord will pass by him. He then experiences a rock-splitting wind, a violent earthquake and an intense fire, none of which were where God was. After these dramatic, powerful, but Divinely empty, encounters, Elijah experiences *dâmam qôl qôl* – a 'silent sound' (the literal translation of the two Hebrew words here) or, as the NRSV puts it, 'a sound of sheer silence' (v. 12). This was where the Divine was! In the silence. Only when Elijah had surrendered his self and began to listen deeply was he able to hear the Divine in the sound of silence.

This wonderful oxymoron of a silent sound gives us insight into the very nature of the Divine and the relationship we can have with the Divine through silence.

John of the Cross says that God spoke one Word, which was Christ, the eternal *Logos*, and that this Word God 'always speaks in eternal silence, and in silence must it be heard by [our] soul'.[4] But what is this Divine silence? This silent word? As Martin Laird tells us:

> It is certainly more than the mere absence of physical sound. More important to realize, however, is that this ineffable reality that the word 'silence' points to is not something that we need to acquire, like a piece of software we can install in the computer of our spiritual lives. It is pointing to something that is already within us.[5]

The Divine silence, the silent sound of the Divine voice, is already within us; we just need to become still and quiet enough within our inner selves to hear this Divine silence. This is the inner journey into the silent land, into what Teresa of Ávila expressed as the centre of the interior castle, the inner journey to the centre of our very being, where the Divine dwells. The doorway to this castle, according to Teresa, is 'prayer and meditation'.[6]

Teresa's interior castle was the very essence of our inner being, our soul: a castle made entirely of clear crystal, in her vision of it, with numerous rooms or mansions where 'in the centre and midst of them all is the chief mansion where the most secret things pass between God and the soul'.[7]

There is a deep wisdom which sits at the heart of the contemplative tradition, a wisdom which, once perceived, though never fully understood, enables us to penetrate all of the froth of life and sink deeply into the Reality who sits at the heart of our being. The wisdom is the sound of Divine silence, and once we perceive that silence at the core of our being, then everything else begins to simply settle into place. Much of our inner discord is due to the internal noise our egos make when they are trying to fathom and control and sort everything out. The discord comes because our egos are noise and the Divine presence is silence, and they cannot occupy the same space at the same time. The noise has to cease before the silence can be experienced.

Once we surrender our ego in obedience to this silence, through practices and 'skills… by which we learn to dispose ourselves to surrender and thus to discover this uncharted land',[8] we can begin to dwell therein. So how do we do that? What practices and skills do we need to have? Teresa of Ávila has already given us two – prayer and meditation. That is the first step through the doorway into the interior castle, into the silent land – prayer and meditation.

In chapter 7 I will be looking more at solitary prayer and the quiet prayer when we are alone, which is, I believe, the prayer which Teresa speaks of. So here let us look at some meditation practices which will help us on the road into the silent land and help us to surrender our egos in obedience to the silent sound at the core of our being.

In chapter 6 of my previous book on Christian meditation, *The Mystic Path of Meditation*,[9] I give some practical suggestions as to how one might set up the right environment for contemplative practices: the setting, sitting positions, creating the appropriate atmosphere, etc. Here, I want to look at two classic practices which have held their own over the centuries, which still aid people into a deep sense of meditation and the presence of silence.

Meditation, the 20th-century Benedictine Swami Bede Griffiths tells us, 'consists in learning to focus and to control the mind… Meditation takes us within ourselves. It is a process of inner withdrawal, a centring in the place of inner detachment, a staying of the mind upon God.'[10]

The first practice I want to look at is one which Griffiths practised for the whole of his monastic life, which is perhaps the oldest consistently used contemplative practice in Christian heritage – the Jesus Prayer. This consists of a short phrase to repeat over and over – 'Lord Jesus Christ, Son of God, have mercy on me' – sometimes including the final phrase, 'a sinner'. After some practice this can be shortened to simply 'Lord, have mercy', but beginning with the full prayer is essential for the focused concentration.

In the fourth century, John Chrysostom said of this prayer: 'It is necessary for everyone, whether eating, drinking, sitting, serving, travelling, or doing anything, to unceasingly cry, "Lord Jesus Christ, Son of God, have mercy on me", that the name of the Lord Jesus Christ, descending into the heart, may subdue the pernicious serpent and save and quicken the soul.'[11] Fifteen hundred years later, after constant use throughout the Eastern/Russian/Coptic Orthodox church, Seraphim of Sarov said of it:

> Let all your attention and training be in [the Jesus Prayer]. Walking, sitting, doing, and standing in church before the divine service, coming in and going out, keep this unceasingly on your lips and in your heart. In calling in this manner on the name of God you will find peace, you will attain to purity of spirit and body, and the Holy Spirit, the Origin of all good things, will dwell in you, and He will guide you into holiness, into all piety and purity.[12]

The idea of the repetitiveness of this prayer, like the use of a prayer bead, is that the words begin to dwell in your heart and your conscious awareness. Therefore, after some practice, the words are no longer needed to be said, internally or externally, from your cognitive self, but they dwell within you and so you are constantly consciously aware of them, like one might be aware of an aroma surrounding them or a ticking clock in the background. The words become a part of your being and so draw you into silence – the Divine silence dwelling within your being. As the current ecumenical patriarch of the Eastern Orthodox church, His All Holiness Bartholomew, says:

> The Jesus Prayer is one way – albeit a powerful and tested way – of preserving the power of silence in prayer. Learning to be silent is far more difficult and far more important than learning to recite prayers. Silence is not the absence of noise but the gift or skill to discern between quiet and stillness. It is the power of learning to listen and the wisdom of learning to know. Silence is a way of being fully involved and active, of being fully alive and compassionate. In prayer, when words end in silence, we awaken to a new awareness and watchfulness. Silence shocks us out of numbness to the world and its needs; it sharpens our vision from its dullness of complacency and selfishness by focusing on the heart of all that matters. Silence is a way of noticing more clearly, of paying attention, and of responding more effectively... Through the Jesus Prayer one develops a greater sense of awareness and attentiveness to the world within and around.[13]

Personally I have been practising the Jesus Prayer for some years using a *chotki*, an Orthodox prayer bead string, which is a bit like the Catholic rosary but a little different in design. I say the prayer as I pass each bead through my fingers. Often, however, I pass the beads through my fingers while practising internal and external silence, but the words of the Jesus Prayer are so interconnected for me with each bead, because of the continued practice, that the 'aroma' of the words dwells in the silence. I also use the beads which hang on the belt of my habit with my Community of Aidan and Hilda cross in this way too.

The second practice I want to look at is slightly younger. It is part of the *Spiritual Exercises* of Ignatius of Loyola. Ignatius was a 16th-century priest who started the Friends of Jesus movement, also known as the Jesuits. He wrote his month-long *Spiritual Exercises* in order to better train people into a deeper communion with the Divine through the three traditional mystic steps of purgation, illumination and unification – becoming one with the Divine. You can still go on residential Ignatian retreats to follow the *Exercises* over the course of a month, most of which is spent in silence. Silence is intrinsically important to the *Exercises*.

The final step of the *Exercises* is the silent contemplation of the love of God. It presents a God who loves without limit and who invites us to make a generous response of love in return. The contemplation invites reflection on four themes:

1 God's gifts to us (life, family, friends, faith, church, eternal life)
2 God's self-giving in Jesus
3 God's continuing work in the world
4 The limitless quality of God's love.

This contemplation is not a cognitive act. It is an act of the higher consciousness of our inner being connecting deeply with the Divine heart and mind, drawing us into a deeper understanding of the love of God. We do not 'think about' these things as much as 'feel' them. This isn't a time for reminiscence or theological exegesis, but of silent reflection and openness to the Divine to reveal to us the deeper reality of these things.

Before we step into the final chapter of this section on silence, I suggest that once again you stop reading, put the book down, and go and be still for a time and go and practise either the Jesus Prayer or the contemplative Ignatian exercise.

6

The wordless way

The sense of speech slowing to a halt in awed wonder before the presence of what is always more than one can say.

Mark McIntosh[1]

The words we use regarding the Divine and the relationship we have with the ineffable have a profound effect on who we are and how our transformative journey progresses. Words, in short, can often be a hindrance. This is where an ancient but lesser-known way of looking at things can help. This way is known as 'apophatic theology'. It can be described as the unknowing of God,[2] a way of relating to the Divine without words or concepts. The following chapter is an edited and adapted version of an essay I wrote as part of my master's degree in Christian spirituality at Sarum College.[3]

In the contemporary western church today there is a great emphasis on cataphatic theology, that is, making positive statements about who God is and what God is like. Many modern worship songs, for example, make bold declarations of who God is. On the surface this may not seem like a bad thing. However, only using cataphatic theology can, in fact, have a negative influence upon the church, both its individuals and the collective universal body. It can detract from the ineffability of the Divine as we create a neat little God we can understand and subsequently create restricted concepts of the Divine which end up becoming the God whom people are taught about, worship and believe in.

Whereas cataphatic theology is the means of discovering or describing God by what God is, apophatic theology is the opposite. The apophatic defines God according to what God is not. This may sound like a strange concept, so let me explain a little.

Thomas Aquinas, a 13th-century Dominican friar, says, 'Having proved the existence of a First Being, which we call God, we have now to examine His nature, i.e. to enquire into the properties of this Being.' He goes on to describe how when scientists or biologists discover a new plant or creature, they first begin to identify it by what it is similar to; however, when it comes to God, 'the Divine essence exceeds in its immensity everything that the human mind can grasp', therefore we cannot identify God by what he is. So, Aquinas says, 'If we cannot attain to what the essence of God is, we can endeavour to ascertain what it is not.'[4] This is essentially what apophatic theology is, or what the 14th-century Dominican friar Meister Eckhart calls the 'doctrine of the no-thingness of God'. As Richard Woods comments:

> A more radical shift in viewpoint [from the teaching of earlier apophatic theologians, such as Aquinas]… finds expression in Eckhart's reciprocal doctrine of the nothingness of God… No one can see God, as John's Gospel has it. For God has no material embodiment to see. God never appears… as an object among other objects, a being among other beings, not even the Supreme Being… God's being is so far beyond human grasp as to seem like nothingness. God is, in this sense, nothing – no *thing*.[5]

Woods continues to say that 'God does not lack being, but wholly transcends it'. Therefore apophatic theology is not *just* about describing God by what he is not, but also about the transcendence of the Divine beyond our understanding – beyond the words and into silence.

The word 'apophatic' comes from the Latin *apophasis* and the Greek *apothazis*, which both mean 'denial'. This denial is a clearing aside of our constructed concepts of God, as the fifth-century Greek mystic Pseudo-Dionysius describes:

> We would be like Sculptors who set out to carve a statue. They remove every obstacle to the pure view of the hidden image, and simply by this act of clearing aside they show up the beauty which is hidden.[6]

This is how the artist and sculptor Michelangelo describes his technique when he says, 'I saw an angel in the marble and carved until I set him free.' He also says, 'In every block of marble I see a statue as plain as though it stood before me, shaped and perfect in attitude and action. I have only to hew away the rough walls that imprison the lovely apparition to reveal it to the other eyes as mine see it.'[7]

In the same way, apophatic theology can clear away all that has been placed around the lovely apparition of God by excessive cataphatic teaching. It can, as Pseudo-Dionysius says, 'remove every obstacle to the pure view of the hidden image' of God, the image of God which is not limited, but, as Michaelangelo says, is 'perfect in attitude and action' and will 'show up the beauty which is hidden'. Once the obstacles are removed, by the deconstruction of the excessive cataphasis, then the 'true' image of the Divine is no longer hidden. This is also true about the words we use to describe God, as Meister Eckhart says:

If one knows anything in God and affixes any name to it, that is not God. God is above names and above nature... We should learn not to give God any name with the idea that we had thereby sufficiently honoured and magnified Him: for God is above names and ineffable.[8]

Even though we need to unname God and understand that he is 'a denial of all names and never had a name',[9] as Eckhart says, cataphasis needs to happen *first* before apophasis can happen. God must be named as something before God can be unnamed. In this process, we must remember that 'negative statements should not be taken as a negative ascription of God's nature, any more than positive terms should be thought able to encapsulate the divine'.[10] This takes us back to Pseudo-Dionysius' statement, echoed by Michelangelo, where we have a kind of deconstruction of our image, or concept, of God to bring us to the 'pure view of the hidden image' and to 'show up the beauty [of God] which is hidden'. It is within this equilibrated tension between the cataphatic and the apophatic that we might find the balance of our naming and unnaming of God, the idea that God is neither one nor the other: that God, in this concept, is in fact no-thing. As Eckhart says: '[God] is pure no-thing: he is neither this nor that. If you think of anything he might be, he is not that.'[11]

Apophasis is a systematic and progressive removal, or stripping away, of each and every concept we have about God in the understanding that they are all inadequate. Oliver Davies explains Eckhart's thoughts as follows:

Passages such as [sermons 54 and 97] show Eckhart's clear preference for speaking of God in radically negative terms, so that nothing is 'added' to him. The inadequacy of using names and affirmative language of God, which conceal rather than reveal him, is to some extent resolved by using negative formulations which appear to subvert the linguistic process itself, and thus God becomes 'nothing of anything' (*nihtes niht*), 'solitude' and 'wilderness' (*einoede, wüestung*) and is 'hidden darkness of the eternal Godhead, which is unknown and never has been known and never shall be known' [sermon 53].[12]

Whatever concept of God we have, as the mystics might say, it is inadequate. Peter Rollins, the Irish philosopher and spiritual teacher, says:

> If we fail to recognize that the term 'God' always falls short of that towards which the word is supposed to point, we will end up bowing down before our own conceptual creations forged from the raw materials of our self-image, rather than bowing before the one who stands over and above that creation. Hence Meister Eckhart famously prays, 'God, rid me of God', a prayer that acknowledges how the God we are in relationship with is bigger, better and different than our understanding of that God.[13]

'The central principle of apophatic discourse is the letting go of the generic name ['God']',[14] or, to put it another way, if we believe our concept of God to actually *be* God, we are in fear of falling into a form of idol worship.

The apophatic teachers make it clear that letting go of the name of God, or unknowing our concept of God, brings us to a greater understanding of who the Divine is. If we are continually overexposed to only cataphatic teaching about God, we are easily led into thinking that our concept of God *is* in actual fact God, or encapsulates the Divine and is adequate as an understanding of God, when it is not and does not, but is only a limited impression. We may even be aware that we only have a concept, but still end up worshipping this concept. If we begin to believe that our own concept of God, the one with which we have been taught by our own stream of church, *is* God in entirety, we can easily fall into the thought-pattern that anyone who sees God differently from us is wrong, because this – what I see as God – is, in fact, God.

This is one of the major causes of denominational division within the modern church – not just what might have caused one stream to split from another initially, but what continues to keep many apart. This is not to suggest that the remedy to this is to abandon denominational doctrine altogether, but that perhaps each stream of church needs to understand that their view of God is just one perspective. One danger of having this singular view of God, as I said, is idol worship. An idol is 'an image or representation of a god used as an object of worship.'[15] Most often this image or representation of a god is made of a physical material – wood, metal or stone – but it is also possible to create such an image within our minds. As the 20th-century Indian Jesuit priest Anthony DeMello says:

> Tragically, people fall into idolatry because they think that where God is concerned, the word [or concept] is the thing [itself]... An internationally famous scripture scholar attended this course in San Francisco, and he said to me, 'My God, after listening to you I understand that I have been an idol worshipper all my life!' He said this openly. 'It never struck me that I had been an idol wor-shipper. My idol was not made of wood or metal; it was a mental idol.' These are the more dangerous idol worshippers. They use a very subtle substance, the mind, to produce their God.[16]

Apophatic theology disables this thought process, as it says that our concept of God is inadequate, that we do not and cannot know the Divine in completeness, as the Divine is ineffable. This means that if others have a different perspective or view of God, that is acceptable, as the Divine is beyond the bounds of our intellectual ken, and so other viewpoints can be just as valid as our own. Here, apophatic theology holds us back from both idol worship and divisive thought and behaviour towards others within the body of Christ.

The apophatic approach enables us to move into higher forms of insight and knowledge, or mystical understandings. By construing language in a manner contrary to that employed within a normal state of consciousness, the possibility of entry into an alternative state of knowing arises. This alternative state of knowing is one which stretches from the heart of Christian mysticism and enables us to know God through unknowing.

Apophasis is not only, therefore, describing God by what God is not, nor simply inclusive of the understanding of the transcendence of the Divine, but it is also the use of paradoxical language to draw us into a place of deeper knowing through unknowing. Paradoxical statements help draw us deeper into the mystery of the ineffability of the Divine. When faced with a paradoxical statement, we become aware of the limitations of the human mind. This creates in us an awareness of the transcendence of the Divine beyond our ken, which in turn makes us receptive to a higher kind of knowledge. This higher kind of knowledge is our soul and spirit's connection with the Divine, gained without sense impressions, images or ideas. According to Mark McIntosh, apophasis happens because:

> Like Moses and the burning bush, persons have been drawn so close to the mystery that they have begun to realize how beautifully, appallingly, heart-breakingly mysterious God really is… Apophasis is the intensifying of desire to such a point that one is left hungering only for the living God – who is of course,

as Aquinas so clearly reminds us, never available as one of the
things that we are capable of grasping, sensing or knowing in
any normal sense.[17]

Apophasis should ultimately lead us to silent contemplation as we
'will finally be at one with him who is indescribable',[18] that which
William James describes as the 'ineffability' aspect of mysticism.[19]
Apophatic theology ends in silence not because we run out of things
to say, as we would in the finite descriptions of a physical object, but,
as McIntosh says in the quotation at the start of this chapter, because
it is 'the sense of speech slowing to a halt in awed wonder before the
presence of what is always more than one can say'.[20]

This is the wordless way of our faith. This is where our silence relates
most deeply with the ineffable Reality.

Part III
Solitude

7

Go to your cell

> The hunger for solitude appears to be the hunger for the gifts
> of solitude: for spiritual and emotional healing, for regaining
> a sense of meaning and purpose, and for getting back in touch
> with ultimate realities. In this sense the hunger for solitude is
> nothing less than a search for God.
>
> Christopher C. Moore[1]

In Luke's gospel, we have what is known as 'the Lord's Prayer'. It begins
with Jesus' disciples witnessing him in prayer, and when he has finished one of his disciples asks for him to teach them how to pray (see
Luke 11:1). I do not believe for one moment that these devout Jews
who followed Jesus were unaware of how they should pray; they
would have been taught how to pray since their early childhood. But
I believe that there was something in the way in which Jesus prayed,
something in how Jesus communicated with the Divine, which was
inspirational and which caught their hearts, captured their imagina-
tion and was awe-inspiring. So when they had finished being witness
to such a wonderful experience, they wanted to know how to com-
mune with the Divine like Jesus did. 'Teach us to pray like *that*!' is
how I read it: 'I thought I knew how to pray, but Jesus, teach us how
to pray like you just did!'

As we have already seen in an earlier chapter, part of Jesus' regular practice in prayer was to go off to quiet places to pray. This, I am sure, was a significant part of forming how Jesus prayed. If we go from Luke's to Matthew's version of Jesus' teaching his disciples the Lord's Prayer, which was obviously a different time to the one recorded in Luke's gospel (all of us who are teachers know that one often has to repeat the same lesson to the same people numerous times before they get it!), we see a very interesting beginning. The first thing which Jesus teaches his disciples about prayer in Matthew's version, and therefore the first teaching by Jesus on prayer that we have in our New Testament, is to go to a quiet solitary place and to use few words (see Matthew 6:6–7). The first thing Jesus teaches his disciples about prayer is what we might term today as solitary contemplative prayer.

This isn't what most people in the modern church often get taught as the first step of prayer. Solitary contemplative prayer might even be seen as a 'higher' form of prayer (if there is such a thing), really only for those who are already quite practised and more deeply spiritual. But this was Jesus' first instruction – solitude and silence (or, at least, not very many words). Only then did he teach the formula, or structure, of basic prayer – the Lord's Prayer:

Acknowledge the Divine, and the hallowedness of Hashem;[2]
Acknowledge our desire for the unfolding of the Divine will;
Acknowledge our need of the Divine;
Acknowledge the inter-relatedness of our actions and Divine
    actions, especially when it comes to forgiveness;
Acknowledge the Divine power over spiritual forces of darkness;
Acknowledge the Ultimate Power and its eternal essence.
Amen!

In desert monasticism, the very beginnings of the monastic tradition from the first few hundred years of Christianity, of which we will discover more in the next chapter, there is a famous statement which reflects the first teaching of Jesus to his disciples about prayer:

> In Scetis a brother went to [Abba] Moses to ask for advice. [Abba Moses] said to him, 'Go and sit in your cell, and your cell will teach you everything.'[3]

The cell was the small domain in which each monk lived. Sometimes two monks would share a cell, literally a 'cell mate', and these were just about big enough for a person to both lay down in and stand up in, and that was about it.

Abba Moses was approached to give advice, which was partly why he was there, but he obviously saw in the person asking that what he needed was simply to follow Jesus' first instruction on prayer: go and sit in a solitary place in silence, and that will teach you everything you need to know. What you need to know you will discover in the silence of solitude. There is a saying – 'everything you need is within you' – and this is true in the sense that the Divine presence dwells within each of us, and that is all we need. We just need to be still and quiet enough to hear the Divine voice. It is this, the Divine presence within us, that we discover when we sit in silent solitude. And this can lead us to such wonderous things.

A contemporary of Abba Moses, Jerome, author of the Vulgate – the Latin translation of the Bible used widely across continental Europe for hundreds of years – wrote of Amma Asella: 'Enclosed in the narrow confines of a single cell she enjoyed the wide pastures of paradise.'[4] Amma Asella 'lived in silence and privacy, appearing discretely in public only when she attended the church of the Holy Martyrs'.[5] In silent solitude she discovered the indwelling Divine presence which led her into the wide pastures of paradise within herself and the enclosed space she was physically in.

In the silence of solitude, we begin to discover and to hear the sound of silence through which the Divine voice 'speaks', just like the prophet Elijah did. In the silence of solitude, we are able to let go of all that distracts and entangles. We are able to let the thoughts in our minds drop away. We are able to be undistracted and to focus fully on the Divine presence.

Solitude is to be alone with the Divine and one's self. 'Each [sister] should be alone in her cell,' says Teresa of Ávila. 'It is easier to keep silence if one is alone, and getting used to solitude is a great help to prayer.'[6]

Each of us can engage in this practice, and some have taken it as a lifestyle. Christian history is full of the stories of solitary hermits who take themselves off to live in the solitude of silence and engage with and encounter the Divine.

One such person was Kevin of Glendalough. He wanted to live a life of a solitary hermit, so he moved into a hollow tree in the valley of two lakes, that is, 'Glen-da-lough', in Ireland. This followed the practice of the early Desert Fathers and Mothers, who went out from the growing urbanisation into the quietness of the desert. However, just as the desert hermits became the beginnings of monastic communities, as people went out to visit them for spiritual direction and eventually began to stay there, so Kevin began to gain people in Glendalough. This became a monastic community.

Kevin, however, still desired solitude, so as the community began to grow he upgraded from a hollow tree to a cave in the side of the cliff overlooking one of the lakes, and finally he built a small stone cell in the woods up the hill a short way away from the main community. Kevin would spend hours and hours in his cell in silent solitude, encountering the Divine presence. Once, so legend says, he stood so long in prayer with his hand out the window of the cell that a blackbird landed upon it and began to build a nest. Such were Kevin's devotions to both long solitary silence and creation that the story says he remained in position so as not to disturb the bird while it nested, laid eggs and fledged her young. An unbelievable, made-up story, you might think – until you look into deeply devotional people such as Sadhu Amar Bharati, a Hindu who has had his arm raised in praise of Shiva since 1973![7] Now one season of a fledging blackbird doesn't seem so long, especially with a windowsill to rest one's arm on.

Despite his community being one of the greatest sites of ancient Celtic monasticism, which is still visitable today, Kevin maintained the desire for solitary silence, knowing that it was a significant aspect of not only his own spiritual and personal growth, but also the growth of the community. The benefits of Kevin's own solitude were poured into the community through his deep encounters with the Divine.

Another great hermit of a similar time was Guthlac, known as the hermit of Crowland, who 'when he heard tell and learned concerning anchorites who of yore longed for the wilderness and hermitages for God's name, and passed their lives there, his heart was inwardly inspired with love of God to long for the wilderness'.[8] Guthlac lived on a small island in the Fens in the East Anglian kingdom during the eighth century. Like many stories of these great early saints, the life of Guthlac is full of battles with demons and spiritual darkness, and divine help from, mostly, St Bartholomew. It was his silence in solitude which enabled him the strength to battle these demons, be they real or 'inner' demons.

We can take encouragement from the life of Guthlac in that, in the times of silent solitude, we can gain the strength from dwelling in the Divine presence to become 'more than conquerors through him who loved us' (Romans 8:37) over the spiritual darkness, in the spirit realms as well as those inner demons we each face.

There are many other hermits throughout the Christian heritage who can inspire us. But it might not feel like something you have a deep desire to do, to go and live as a solitary hermit. Your heart might not be 'inwardly inspired with love of God to long for the wilderness', like Guthlac's was. But perhaps there is a desire in you to take some time out for a short period, to have your own space.

There is a growing desire in western culture for solitude, for taking time out at least, if not becoming a full hermit. The desire to 'have one's own space' is a real and, I would say, necessary desire which comes from a deeply primal part of our true being. Christopher C. Moore says:

This use of the word 'space' to denote a kind of personal psychological enclave has an interesting and revealing history. It first appeared in the [English] language in the mid 1300s and remained in common usage for three hundred years until the mid 1600s, when it disappeared. As recently as 1983, the ninth edition of *Webster's New Collegiate Dictionary* listed ten definitions of 'space', none of them denoting the psychological dimension. However, in the tenth edition, a new definition of space was added: 'The opportunity to assert or experience one's identity or needs freely.' Why would a particular definition of a word, obsolete for three centuries, suddenly reappear in the language? The answer is obvious: because the concept embodied by that usage has once again become relevant to large numbers of people. It is in the concept of 'needing one's own space' that we find an inchoate and unconscious longing for solitude.[9]

We all feel the need for our own space on occasion. Perhaps not as a lifestyle, like the solitary hermits, but at least to take time out to just be alone – to go to our cell and experience the wide pastures of paradise within ourselves.

This is different from taking a communal retreat, which we spoke of in an earlier chapter; this is about solitude and being intentionally alone. This is about being alone in the Divine presence so as to hear the silence for ourselves, on our own. Do you ever feel this desire? If so, there are some very simple things you can do. One is to simply clear a space in your diary, switch everything off in your own home which could cause distractions, such as your mobile phone, and just be in the stillness and the silence. You may need to practise this to get used to it, and you may need to use some meditation techniques to get your thoughts to become still, but after a while, the silence of solitude will become a home in which you feel comfort and warmth. You may even try hiring a small one-bedroom cottage somewhere isolated and spend a few days there with the intention of spending much of that time in silent solitude. Or perhaps you could find a local Christian retreat centre where you can have some solitude, or a local monastic centre which might offer you some space.

Another way to engage in this is to find a solitary place outside in nature. This might take a bit more organising and working out, as people can be everywhere, but there are places that one can go where you can engage in solitary silence. Engaging in intentional solitary silence in the natural world brings a whole new level of experience to your practice.

I have engaged in silent solitude in all of the above examples, and I have learned that one's experience is different depending upon where one engages in this practice. Try more than one, and perhaps you will even think of more examples and find new places to be alone dwelling in the Divine presence in silence.

So, following the instructions and examples of the Desert Fathers and Mothers, and the words of Christ: go to your cell, find a solitary space, be silent, or at least use very few words, and just be. Perhaps you will discover the beautiful pastures of paradise within.

Do this now. Once again, put this book down, and create the space for at least a short practice of silent solitude. Go to your cell and your cell will teach you everything. Do this 'for spiritual and emotional healing, for regaining a sense of meaning and purpose, and for getting back in touch with Ultimate Realities'.[10]

8

The desert of your heart

What the [Desert Fathers and Mothers] sought most of all was their own true self, in Christ. And in order to do this, they had to reject completely the false, formal self, fabricated under social compulsion in 'the world'. They sought a way to God that was uncharted and freely chosen, not inherited from others who had mapped it out beforehand. They sought a God whom they alone could find, not one who was 'given' in a set, stereotyped form from somebody else.

Thomas Merton[1]

In the early centuries of Christianity there was what we might today call a movement. It began during the persecutions in the third century and continued through the early years of the legalisation of Christianity by Emperor Constantine in the early fourth century. This movement was of men and women moving out of the cities and into the deserts in the Middle East and Egypt to be solitary hermits and to live wholly for God. These people are known as the Desert Fathers and Mothers. We met a couple of them in the previous chapter.

Some of these individuals moved out into the desert to escape the persecution of Christians, but after Christianity was legalised across the Roman Empire, some moved out into the desert to live a more authentic life dedicated to the Divine. After Constantine legalised Christianity, he began to give concessions to priests with regards to taxes, housing and other things, which caused a number of people to start to become priests who had previously not had any interest in the Christian faith. The 'state church' began to develop and became much more political than spiritual. Many people, especially those who had stood firm in their faith during the persecutions, found this unacceptable, and so moved out of the cities, away from the growing institutionalisation and sanitisation of the church, and into the desert in solitude to live in greater austerity and dedication to their faith.

These individuals soon began to gather others around them, and this became the beginnings of monasticism. The reason these individuals drew others to them was because of their holiness and their teaching. There is a good amount of their teachings and life examples available to us still. The sayings and lives of the Desert Fathers and Mothers have become famous and deeply directional all through the ages. Mainly via John Cassian and Martin of Tours, desert monasticism was one of the major influences on Celtic Christianity in Britain and Ireland, and is a huge part of the heritage of the Eastern Orthodox Church and their spiritual life guidance book *The Philokalia*. We expanded on one single statement in the previous chapter, and in this one we will look at a few more through which we might be able to better navigate and live in the desert of our heart, our own inner place of being more authentic and devoted in our faith to the Divine.

As we step into a few sayings of the Desert Fathers and Mothers, it is worth a small introduction. Thomas Merton, a monk from the 20th century, taught and wrote a lot about desert monasticism. He says that the Desert Fathers and Mothers:

… were in a certain sense 'anarchists', and it will do no harm to think of them in that light. They were [people] who did not believe in letting themselves be passively guided and ruled by a decadent state, and who believed that there was a way of getting along without slavish dependence on accepted, conventional values… They were humble, quiet, sensible people, with a deep knowledge of human nature and enough understanding of the things of God to realize that they knew very little about Him.[2]

In her book on forgotten Desert Mothers, Laura Swan says:

Desert ascetics cultivated a heart engaged in intense listening. Listening for the Beloved's voice cultivated a wise and compassionate heart, able to yield to the movements of the Holy Spirit. Listening to the ebbs and flows of the Spirit was fundamental to a life of discernment. A still, focused attention was needed for fruitful discernment. True discernment does not presuppose how the Spirit will move, nor what God will say. In this life of cultivated listening, [these desert] ascetics were open to the unexpected. They were willing to be surprised [by God].[3]

So what do these ancient men and women from the first few centuries have to teach us in our modern lives? What have they to say to our pursuit of the art of peace? What do these first Christian mystics have in their wisdom which will help us when we enter the desert of our heart?

Let us read carefully the following wisdom and discover the Divine light shining still from those ancient deserts:

Evagrius said, 'Cut the desire of a multitude of things from your heart, and stop your mind being distracted, and therefore your stillness lost.'

Nilus said, 'The arrows of the enemy cannot affect those who love quiet, but those who are distracted by the crowds will often feel the arrows strike.'

There were once three friends who decided to become monks. One of them decided that he would follow Matthew 5:9 and endeavour to make peace among people; the second decided he would follow Matthew 25:34–40 and endeavour to heal the sick and feed the hungry; the third decided to follow Luke 5:16 and go into the desert to be in silence. After a time, the first monk found that he became despondent in his heart, as he was unable to settle all quarrels, and many people would not listen to him and did not want peace, so he went to the one tending the sick and the poor. He found that this monk too was despondent in heart, as he was unable to make much difference to the great need. The two of them decided to go to the one in the desert who sat in silence. When they got to him, they asked how he was doing in his calling. This third monk sat silent for a while and then poured a jug of water into a large bowl. 'Look into the water,' he said to his companions. They looked and could not see clearly as the water was disturbed and agitated, not yet settled. They sat back down waiting. The three sat in silence and stillness for a while. Finally the monk who had poured the water said to them, 'Look again into the water.' The two did so again, and this time they saw clearly their own reflections. They sat back down and looked at the monk who had poured the water, who looked up to them and said, 'So it is with each of us. We must become still and quiet for us to clearly see our true selves, and thus know what we are called to do in the Divine image.'

Some brothers asked Macarius, 'How should we pray?' Macarius replied, 'There is no need for many words in your prayers. Reach out your hands in silence and open your heart and say, "Lord, have mercy upon me", but if inner conflict troubles you say, "Lord, help me in your will." For God knows what is best for us and has mercy.'

It is said of Abba Agatho that for three years he held a stone in his mouth until he was able to control his tongue in silence.

One of the elders in a certain place taught that the monk's cell was like the fiery furnace in which the Holy Three stood with the Divine, but it is also like the cloud out of which the Divine spoke to Moses.

A young brother came to Abba Pastor and told him that many distracting thoughts come into his head during contemplation, and asked how he might stop them. Abba Pastor thrust the young brother out of his cell into the desert wind and said, 'Open your cloak and catch the wind to stop it.' 'This I cannot do,' the young brother replied. 'As much as you cannot catch the wind and stop it, you cannot catch or stop the thoughts coming into your mind. You simply must say no, refuse to engage with them.'

One of the elders of a certain place said, 'Apply yourself to silence... and be intent in meditation, then whether you sit quietly or work... you will not have to fear the attacks of the evil one.'

Amma Matrons said, 'We take ourselves wherever we go, we cannot get away from our temptations simply by going to another place.'

Amma Syncletica said, 'As medicine which is bitter to the taste drives out the poison of illness, so the disciplines of prayer and fasting drive out evil thoughts.'

Before you read on, I am going to suggest that you once again put this book down, take one of the above statements, the one which resonated with you the most, and go and sit in a quiet place and contemplate it. Engage in the ancient contemplative practice of Lectio Divina with it. Lectio Divina is usually practised with a small section of scripture, but can be just as effective when used with some wisdom from others within the Christian heritage. If you have never practised Lectio Divina before, then let me explain it for you. There are four stages to traditional Lectio Divina, although I usually add a fifth.

Read (*lectio*)
Slowly begin reading your chosen short passage, savouring each word and phrase. Read and reread the same passage or verse over and over again. Stay with it. Just keep reading it over and over.

Reflect (*meditatio*)
Put the book down and allow the words to dwell in your mind and inner being. Ponder the words, but try not to think cognitively about what the passage might be saying. Just simply allow a sense of it to arise within you. Let the words sink deeper and deeper, through all the layers of your being. Listen for what these words say to you within the circumstances of your current life. What gifts do these words offer you? What insights arise to the surface of your heart?

Respond (*oratio*)
Oratio is spoken prayer. Express to the Divine what is within your heart in words of gratitude, petition, praise or lament. Be honest. You may want to respond aloud, or you may want to speak silently to the Divine

within your heart. You might want to write down your thoughts; recording them in a journal can be useful when looked back on in the future.

Rest (*contemplatio*)

After a short time of reflecting on the words – only you will know when the right time is, so follow the natural feel within you – let go of all your thoughts and all the words. Surrender the words on which you have been meditating. Allow yourself to rest silently in Divine love and peace. Allow the Divine to bring things to your heart and mind. Let the Divine speak to you about the words you have been reflecting on. But again, don't think: just let these things arise within your inner being.

Relate (*dictu*)

I use the Latin word *dictu* for my fifth extra stage here, which means 'in the telling', because it is in our everyday lives that we find out whether or not the words and meditations have sunk into our being and become a part of who we are. It is no good reading the Bible, or other sacred texts, even if you hear the Divine voice, if you do not relate it to the way you live your life. We are not talking here about applying religious rules and doctrine to your life or trying to 'be good', or even trying to be a 'good' Christian. Instead, this is about taking the particular aspects which you have gained from the words you have meditated upon with you throughout the day and allowing them to continue to work in your mind and heart. See how it applies to the daily circumstances of your life. Allow it to interweave through the hours of your everyday life as it weaves into the very fabric of your being.

So now you have the outline of Lectio Divina, put this book down, take one of the above statements, the one which resonated with you the most, and go and sit in a quiet place and contemplate it. Engage in the ancient contemplative practice of Lectio Divina with it.

Welcome back.

A final word before we finish this chapter – a word on the desert of our heart.

All the ontology of desert monasticism can be embodied in our own journey as we retreat to the desert of our heart. Not many of us will be called to physically find a place to live in solitude like the Desert Fathers and Mothers. Not many of us will feel the call to disconnect physically with the societal culture into which we are so intrinsically interwoven, but many of us will indeed feel a draw to disconnect with it occasionally. So we can withdraw into our own heart, into our own inner being, in the same way that those of ancient times withdrew physically to the deserts.

Our inner being, the very core of our 'selves', our heart, is a place which needs the cultivation of the silence of the desert and the intense listening which Laura Swan speaks of in her book on the Desert Mothers. Through this occasional withdrawal into the desert of our heart, we do not 'presuppose how the Spirit will move, nor what God will say', but 'in this life of cultivated listening, [we are] open to the unexpected. [We are] willing to be surprised [by God].'[4]

In the desert of our heart, we encounter a more transcendent Reality, just as the Desert Fathers and Mothers did. This Reality, the Divine Reality, enables us to better overcome the temptations and darkness which we may encounter in our normal, everyday lives.

9

Alone together

Let him who cannot be alone beware of community. Let him who is not in community beware of being alone... Each by itself has profound pitfalls and perils. One who wants fellowship without solitude plunges into the void of words and feelings, and one who seeks solitude without fellowship perishes in the abyss of vanity, self-infatuation, and despair... Blessed is he who is alone in the strength of the fellowship and blessed is he who keeps the fellowship in the strength of aloneness.
Dietrich Bonhoeffer[1]

The contemplative life is a wonderful way to spend time alone in the Divine presence in peace and tranquillity, building up an inner environment which you then live out, as we have seen so far. However, there is a difference between living this practice alone and living it with others, and a very special experience of living it alone together.

In the previous two chapters we looked at desert monasticism and time alone in solitude. However, as Laura Swan says:

Monasticism is a communal endeavour. The story of a monastic woman is also the story of her community. Many of the first monastic communities evolved around a single charismatic personality. Others were complex webs of relationships among many gifted women. Many monasteries included hermits; others were in close contact with desert ascetics.[2]

In historical and traditional monasticism, the 'alone together' concept was called the *laura* way of monasticism. Although the term *laura* has been almost exclusively used historically with regards to the early monastic centres in Palestine, the type of monastery which it describes existed not only there, but in Syria, Mesopotamia, Gaul and Italy, and among the Celtic monks. The type of life led there might be described as something midway between purely eremitical (solitary) and purely cenobitical (communal) life. The monk lived alone, though depended on a superior and visited them, but was also bound to the communal life on Saturdays and Sundays, when all met in church for the solemn eucharistic liturgy.

In this chapter, I want to expand a little upon the monastic tradition and look at a modern appropriation of it – New Monasticism. Essentially I want to look at being alone together. But what do I mean by 'alone together'? Is that not a contradiction? Hopefully by now you will have picked up that oxymorons and paradoxes are part and parcel of mysticism. And here is another one: alone together.

This is, in fact, the essence of the monastic life. One simply has to look at the etymology of the word 'monk' to see this:

From Old English *munuc* (used also of women), from Proto-Germanic *muniko-* (source also of Old Frisian *munek*, Middle Dutch *monic*, Old High German *munih*, German *Mönch*), an early borrowing from Vulgar Latin *monicus* (source of French *moine*, Spanish *monje*, Italian *monaco*), from Late Latin *mona-chus* 'monk', originally 'religious hermit,' from Ecclesiastical

> Greek *monakhos* 'monk', noun use of a classical Greek adjective meaning 'solitary,' from *monos* 'alone'.[3]

Yet when we think of monks, we think of them not as alone, but as a community in a monastery – what are known as cenobites. 'Cenobite' comes from the Latin *coenobita*, meaning 'a cloister brother', and from the Greek *koinobiont*, meaning 'life in community'. These kinds of monks, according to Benedict, founder of the Benedictine Order, are 'the strongest kind of monks';[4] these, along with the less common *laura* monks, were all finding strength in being alone together.

Monasticism is the perfect balance of aloneness and togetherness: of living alone together, like the togetherness and connectedness of the centre and circumference of a circle. As is true with almost everything in life, balance is the key. Esther de Waal says:

> Balance, proportion, harmony are so central, they so underpin everything in the Rule, that without them the whole Benedictine approach to the individual and to the community loses its keystone... Thus the idea of order and balance runs through the organization of the monastery.[5]

What we discover in monastic living (in which, like the Old English word *munuc* did, I include women) is a group of individuals living in the balance of being alone together, that is, gaining the benefits of the solitary times without losing the benefits of community belonging. We are not designed, in fact, to live solely alone, unless we are specifically called by the Divine to be a solitary hermit, which very few are. Irish mystic John O'Donohue says:

> The hunger to belong is at the heart of our nature. Cut off from others we atrophy and turn in on ourselves... Our hunger to

belong is the longing to bridge the gulf that exists between isolation and intimacy... Everyone longs for intimacy and dreams of a nest of belonging in which one is embraced, seen and loved. Something within each of us cries out for belonging.[6]

The balance between what my friend calls 'peopleing' and 'not people-ing' is essential to our mental well-being. We must learn to be alone together, to find solitude in the balance of community, as the wonderful prayer by Andy Raine from the Northumbria Community says, follow-ing the feel of the rhythm of the tides on the Holy Island of Lindisfarne:

Leave me alone with God as much as may be. As the tide draws the waters close in upon the shore, make me an island, set apart, alone with you, God, holy to you. Then with the turning of the tide prepare me to carry your presence to the busy world beyond, the world that rushes in on me till the waters come again and fold me back to you.[7]

As well as this, we need to understand the benefit of communal silence. There is a difference between sitting in silence alone and sit-ting in silence together – like the difference you can feel between being in a house alone and being in a house when someone else is there. Even if they are in a different room or on a different floor, one can feel the difference. The energy created in collective silence is different from that created when one is in silence alone, and so it actually affects us differently.

The collective who perhaps most commonly embody this outside of monastic centres are the Quakers, the Religious Society of Friends. Their usual weekly gathering is held mostly in silence. While most people go to church each week and sing songs passionately and lis-ten to lots of words being said, the Quakers' form of worship is silent waiting – collective silent waiting. In the section on Silent Waiting in their book of Quaker disciplines, it says:

> Meeting is the chance to escape from the trivial thoughts of everyday living, and to find answers from yourself and from God. Some people are scared of the silence… Don't feel restricted by the silence, it is there to set you free from the pressures of life… We highly prize silent waiting upon the Lord in humble dependence upon him. We esteem it to be a precious part of spiritual worship, and trust that no vocal offering will ever exclude it from its true place in our religious meeting.[8]

If you struggle to sit quietly alone, then perhaps you might try collective silence. Perhaps you might find a way to be alone together with others: a local Quaker meeting house, a local meditation group or perhaps a local monastic centre which allows the public to join in with their prayer rhythms and sit alone, together in silence. The aim is to be still in your own space and own mind, but also to benefit from the collective energy of others around you.

Another way of doing this is being discovered by many people around the globe these days through what is known as New Monasticism.

New Monasticism is a movement of lay people who are finding benefit in creating life with the framework of a monastic Rule or Way of Life. Similarly to the traditional Third Orders, New Monastic orders or communities are made up of people living out their chosen monastic Rule in their usual everyday life. Unlike the Third Orders, they do not directly link with a traditional First Order (such as the Franciscans or Benedictines). New Monastic communities create their Rule from other sources. The New Monastic community I belong to, for example, the Community of Aidan and Hilda, creates its Way of Life by gleaning what we can from the historical Celtic monastic rules from the fourth to ninth centuries in Britain and Ireland. New Monastic communities 'envision a community in which the devotional disciplines that nurtured the radical spirituality of traditional monks are reinterpreted so that the Christian community can participate in the performance of the melodies of God in the midst of contemporary society'.[9] There is a change afoot, a shift happening in the consciousness of many Christians. Stuart Burns of Mucknell Abbey says:

> The era of Christendom is over, however much many church-going Christians may not recognize or wish to admit it... By the Middle Ages, church and state had become twin pillars... This is no longer true and the great institutions of that era are now crumbling, if they haven't already disappeared. We are on the threshold of a new era and a new paradigm is beginning to emerge... These expressions of Christian New Monasticism are attempts to live the Christian gospel with a fresh integrity.[10]

This paradigm shift comes as part of a natural 500-year(ish) rhythm of structural change in the universal church. 500 years from Christ was the rise of the Latin church through Europe and the decline of the Celtic monastic tradition; 500 years after that was the great schism of east and west; 500 years after that was the Reformation; 500 years after that is now![11]

Like the Desert Fathers and Mothers, whom we met in the previous two chapters, people are feeling the need to escape the mainstream institution called 'church', as they are finding that it is not giving or living what is needed, and sometimes not even living the gospel of Christ at all. But, still being Christ-centred in their spiritual life, they are finding a home and an affinity within New Monastic communities. These are non-residential communities, meaning that when one joins a community one doesn't move into a monastic centre, but they understand that the world is their monastery.[12]

This isn't necessarily, though, an 'either or' situation. You don't have to choose between traditional church or New Monasticism, although some have. But, just as traditional monasticism has always been connected to the universal church yet outside of it, so New Monasticism wishes to create a catalyst of difference in life attitude and expectancy of Christian living to what might be presented in much of traditional modern church teaching.

One thing that the Covid-19 crisis of 2020–21 showed, to the shock of many, I am sure, was that one could still be a Christian even if one didn't get to go to a building once a week. There was a rise in understanding that Christianity is a way of life, and not just a set of rules to follow which are encouraged through sermons on Sunday mornings. New Monasticism has this Way of Life at its core, whereas traditional church has the weekly gathering at its core.

As I have said already, balance is the key: a balance of gathering with other like-minded people (rhythm and day is irrelevant) and of being alone, living out the Way of Life. As the quotation from Bonhoeffer at the start of this chapter says, 'Let him who cannot be alone beware of community. Let him who is not in community beware of being alone… Blessed is he who is alone in the strength of the fellowship and blessed is he who keeps the fellowship in the strength of aloneness.'[13] New Monasticism helps individuals find that balance.

Creating a Way of Life is at the heart of New Monasticism. In the Community of Aidan and Hilda, we have a Rule based on our own appropriation of the three basic principles of monasticism, and then ten elements that create the Way of Life which each member lives.

However, each member is encouraged to expand upon each point so that it reflects them as individuals, and can be lived out as a life-giving aspect of their everyday life and not become a burden. Certainly the Way of Life should not just be a to-do list.

Here I will briefly unpack the Way of Life of the Community of Aidan and Hilda as an example.[14] As a completely dispersed community, right around the globe, local connection is not an overly emphasised aspect, although each set of members in close physical proximity to one another are encouraged to meet together regularly. We have local area groups, each with its own local area coordinator. But unlike some other New Monastic communities, we practise living alone together through each member of the Community living out the Rule and keeping the daily prayer rhythms. Knowing that others are living this Way of Life and praying at the same times as you, despite you being alone, brings a sense of community and togetherness. It is a connection in a higher state than simply physical proximity.

The three traditional monastic principles are poverty, chastity and obedience. The Community of Aidan and Hilda have slightly adapted these both to better suit a dispersed non-residential community and to better reflect Celtic monastic practice.

Instead of poverty we have simplicity. If you are going to move into a monastic centre, then to give up everything one owns is possible, but if one is going to continue to live in one's own house in the world, that is not possible. However, through our principle of simplicity we make a conscious choice to live contrary to consumerism and materialism, and to intentionally live a conscientious life in what we have and buy. We are aware of what we have, whether it be a little or a lot, and we are conscious that it all belongs to God and is gifted to us to steward for a time.

We have replaced chastity with purity. Again, living in the world with our families we felt a slight adjustment was needed. Even within Celtic monastic centres historically there were married monks (men and women). But in purity we hold our whole physical being, including our sexuality and sexual activity, before the Divine and hold it as sacred.

We kept obedience the same, as this was and is about obedience to God and to the Rule to which you feel called to commit to. And as we discovered in chapter 5, this is about a deep listening.

In a short summary of each of the ten elements of the Way of Life, I share here what members of the Community of Aidan and Hilda commit to:

1 **Lifelong learning** – Knowing that we will never know it all, we commit to continue our learning through scripture and the lives of the Celtic and others saints through the ages, as well as through the natural world and an experiential relationship with the Divine.

2 **Spiritual journey** – Alongside a Soul Friend (Anam Cara) for guidance and wisdom, we travel lightly along life's path, understanding that we will never fully 'arrive' while we embody the physical form, but that we always travel with friends and those around us who are not yet friends.

3 **A rhythm of prayer, work and re-creation** – Keeping in line with traditional monasticism, we keep hours of prayer – morning, midday, evening and night. By punctuating the day with specific intentional stops of prayer and focus, it is easier to engage with the struggles and joys of life. This doesn't stop us praying at any other time, but it does ensure that prayer flows through our

whole day. This rhythm also ensures that our work–life balance is kept right, as we commit to neither overwork nor being slothful. But we do the work we are called to do (paid or unpaid) and also engage with those things which bring us life and re-create our inner being.

4 **Initiating God's will in God's world** – This element used to be called 'intercession', but we found that so many people had different understandings of that word, so we changed it. We endeavour to pray for and initiate the Divine will within the local 'world' into which we are called to live. We sometimes use the phrase, 'Bloom where you are planted.'

5 **Simple lifestyle** – This expands from the basic monastic principle, and we look to the phrase, 'Live simply, so that others may simply live,' which should inform our whole being and lifestyle.

6 **Care for creation** – In Celtic Christianity there was no separation between the physical and the spiritual; everything was spiritual. The earth is a beautiful place saturated by the Divine presence and imbued with it. The very essence of the Divine flows through it, and it is something which God loves enough to die for (note that the word 'world' in John 3:16 is the Greek word *kosmos*, which means the whole created order, not just humans). Therefore we should respond and act towards it in light of this. If we understand that to share the gospel is more than simply speaking words to people, but is about how we live our lives, then the command of Christ to 'preach the gospel to all creation' (Mark 16:15) includes the way we treat the earth and the world we live in.

7 **Healing fragmented people and communities** – We are committed to being part of the healing of the brokenness of the world,

both in its individuals and in its larger communities – bringing the Divine balm of Shalom to all.

8 **Openness to God's Spirit** – A modern perspective of the Holy Spirit in Celtic Christianity is the Wild Goose. Although this symbol cannot be traced back further than George MacLeod, the founder of the Iona Community in the 1930s, it does reflect the way that historical Celtic Christians understood the Divine Spirit – wild, untameable and unpredictable, not a nice white fluffy dove (which, incidentally was not the kind of wild Middle Eastern rock dove which landed on Jesus' head at his baptism). We are committed to being open to this Wild Goose, wherever that might lead us.

9 **Unity** – 'That all of them may be one... so that the world may believe' (John 17:21). These are Jesus' words for all future believers (so, you and I) while he was praying just before his crucifixion. If we wish the world to believe in the Cosmic Christ and the eternal and universal work of the cross, then we, the global body of Christ, need to be one – unified as the church. Therefore all members of the Community of Aidan and Hilda, as a fully ecumenical community, are committed to ecumenicalism and, as much as we each can, drawing the divisions between churches together and into one.

10 **Mission** – We are committed to bringing the true gospel of Love and the Divine kingdom to the world in which we live and to the lives of those we are called to encounter. We do this mostly through life example, but also taking the Divinely orchestrated opportunities which are placed before us to speak and share in whatever other way appropriate to the gospel of Christ and the Divine kingdom.

In living this out as individuals, we express our own devotion to our personal calling. But knowing that every individual member of the Community is also living this out enables us to be alone together with all other members of our New Monastic community around the world. We may sometimes be alone, but we are alone together.

Part IV

Sanctuary

10

Seeking refuge

Elohim is our refuge and strength, a very present help in trouble. Therefore we will not fear, though the earth should change... YHWH t'shaw-baw is with us; Elohim of Israel is our refuge.

The Korahites[1]

I have entitled this final section of the book 'Sanctuary'. This is because we sometimes need to find sacred, safe spaces in certain times of our contemplative practice and life. We need sanctuary.

The word 'sanctuary' comes from the Anglo-French *sentuarie*, and the Old French *saintuaire*, which means 'sacred relic, holy thing; reliquary, sanctuary'. These come from the Late Latin *sanctuarium*, 'a sacred place, shrine' (especially related to the Hebrew Holy of Holies or sanctum), all of which come from the Latin *sanctus*, meaning 'holy', from which we get the word 'saint'.[2]

A sanctuary is a holy place, yet also a place of refuge, thanks to a law of Emperor Constantine, later established more specifically in the Middle Ages in England, relating to criminals being able to avoid arrest for most crimes by seeking refuge in church buildings, which were holy places and so not a place for forced arrests.

When we seek sanctuary, we are seeking a place of holiness and safety; we are seeking to escape the world and to find a place of Divine presence. But where do we find these? And are they necessary for the mystic when engaging in contemplation?

If you have been practising contemplation for any length of time, you will know that there are times when you feel in total desolation, when the Divine presence seems to have disappeared totally, and when you feel alone. It is in these times when we might feel we need sanctuary. But where can sanctuary be found? In a church building, like the criminals of old? Perhaps. They can often be places of quiet stillness. In nature? Definitely; see a long expansion of this in the next chapter. But what if you can't get to either of these places? Or anywhere else where you might feel safe. What if there is no choice but to be where you are? What then?

These are the times when the contemplative practice you had been doing in times of consolation can be life-saving.

In the continued practice of contemplation, we create the inner environment for the Divine to dwell, such that we are able to know beyond knowledge that we abide in the Divine and the Divine abides in us. In our continued practice we create the inner environment where we can seek and find that which is our true self; we create a pathway to what the mystics call the ground of our being, or the ground of our soul, which is the Divine presence itself dwelling within us, where it has always been. We just needed to create the inner environment where we could experience it and have it shine out from the core of our being to every tiny corner of who we are.

In short, we can find this refuge within ourselves, as the Divine presence is within us, and we, in our times of consolation, have created the pathway which leads us there. As I have said already in this book, everything you have is within you, because the Divine is already within you, and all you need is the Divine.

So the Divine within us can be our refuge and our strength, as the psalm at the start of this chapter says, a very present help in times of trouble. Therefore we have no need to fear; though the 'earth should change' or we find ourselves in time of desolation, we know that the Divine is with us and is our refuge, our sanctuary.

But what might have caused this time of desolation? Why might we have begun to feel like this?

Of course, each person practising contemplation is only a person, so is fallible and liable to fall to various temptations on the contemplative path – egotistic projection; boredom; distraction, both internal and external; and other things which might cause our inner being to feel in disequilibrium and unable to connect with the Divine. But I want to look at four particular reasons why, in the contemplative practice, these feelings might arise. These are taken from the writings of four mystics of our heritage – Meister Eckhart, the author of *The Cloud of Unknowing*, John of the Cross and Anthony DeMello, who speak, respectively, on attachment, the attacks and negative comments from others, the dark night of the senses and an empty void in prayer. The first two are things we might bring on ourselves; the latter two are things the Divine draws us through to go into deeper contemplation.

Attachment

We start, then, with Meister Eckhart and his teaching on attachment, or more accurately, on *de*tachment. In some of his sermons of which we have transcripts, Eckhart taught on detachment, but he also wrote a short paper specifically on the subject. He spent time studying various Christian and non-Christian papers and books to discover 'which is the best and highest virtue whereby a man may chiefly and most firmly join himself to God'.[3] Through his study he came to the conclusion that 'only pure detachment surpasses all things, for all virtues have some regard to [things], but detachment is free of [that]… he who would be serene and pure needs but one thing: detachment'.[4]

Eckhart says that our attachment to things can draw us away from the Divine and can cause divided loyalties. This isn't to say that we should not have things or other people in our lives, but that we need to ensure that we hold all things lightly and that we do not become overly attached to them in a way that they begin to come before the Divine in our lives and the path which unfolds before us. We should not become 'full' of these things. For 'to be empty of all [things] is to be full of God, and to be full of all [things] is to be empty of God'.[5]

Eckhart's teaching here is similar to what Jesus said about not being able to have two masters, else we will 'hate the one and love the other, or… be devoted to the one and despise the other' (Matthew 6:24). Because, as Eckhart says:

> In whatever heart there is this or that. There may be something in 'this' or 'that' which God cannot bring to the highest peak. And so, if the heart is to be ready to receive the highest, it must rest on absolutely nothing, and in that lies the greatest potentiality which can exist. For when the detached heart rests in the highest, that can only be on nothing, since that has the greatest receptivity… Therefore, the quicker a man flees from [things] the quicker the Creator runs towards him… That is why detachment is best, it purifies the soul, purges the conscience, kindles the

heart, awakens the spirit, quickens the desire, makes us know
God and, cutting off [things], unites us with God.[6]

If we are feeling that we are in a time of desolation, perhaps we have
formed an attachment to something which is hindering the Divine
work within us. Seek refuge in the Divine presence within to discover
whether this is the case.

Attacks and negative comments from others

If we have not formed any attachment to anything, then perhaps we
are feeling that we are in a time of desolation because others have
put us down and spoken against us and we have taken these words
to heart. Perhaps we are even expending energy trying to defend
ourselves against these people and their words. *The Cloud of Unknowing* calls these people 'actives', that is, those who think that the contemplative life and practice is a waste of time and that we should be
getting on with doing something!

Such negative words were directed at me not so long ago. When I spoke
of the importance of making time to intentionally do nothing, one person responded, 'The cry should be to do something, to be an activist,
to shout out for those in need. In my humble opinion an hour's activity
volunteering at a food bank, Citizens Advice or whatever is more beneficial than an hour's meditation. To do nothing or to do something?
Do something always.' We can easily take these attacks personally, feel
the hurt which such words can bring and feel the need to defend our
position, which can easily lead us into a place of desolation. Throughout a number of chapters from the late teens to early twenties in *The
Cloud of Unknowing*, the author uses the story of Mary and Martha as
an illustration for such negativity towards the contemplative.

In this story (Luke 10:38–42), Jesus has come to visit a house in which Mary and Martha live. Mary is sitting at Jesus' feet listening to what he has to say. Martha is 'worried and upset about many things'. Martha moans about Mary to Jesus. She sees that Mary is just sitting in the Divine presence while there are things to be done which she, Martha, is getting on with doing.

> Martha complained about her sister. When Martha demanded that our loving, omniscient Lord Jesus sit in judgement on Mary, he didn't. He could have turned right around and demanded that she get up and help Martha serve him, but he did better than that. He saw that Mary was so absorbed in loving him and contemplating his divinity that she would not stop, even to defend herself, so in his usual gentle manner, he answered for her, reasoning with Martha. He became Mary's advocate and defended her for loving him.[7]

Mary was subject to the kind of words that I, and many of us, hear from the 'actives', but she, like I when I received the words I mentioned above, did not waver from the contemplative path. She did not even turn her eyes away from Jesus, but just carried on. And Jesus himself defended her. The chapter that the above quotation comes from in *The Cloud of Unknowing* is actually called 'How the all-powerful God well defends those who won't stop loving him through contemplative prayer to stick up for themselves'.

If we are feeling that we are in a time of desolation, perhaps we have been subject to negative words or attacks from others and they have wounded us, or we are trying to defend ourselves when really we need to leave that to the Divine. Seek refuge in the Divine presence within to discover whether this is the case. (See chapter 12 for my counter-balance showing that it is not all about just sitting and contemplating at the expense of the practical social action.)

The dark night of the senses

The third reason that we might be feeling that we are in a time of desolation is what John of the Cross calls the 'dark night of the senses'. Unlike the first two reasons, this (and the next one) are actually about the Divine path drawing us deeper.

St John of the Cross wrote a poem called *The Dark Night of the Soul*, which has mistakenly become a phrase that many use to refer to a hard or horrible period that they go through. But this is not what John meant by it at all. But before we arrive at the dark night of the soul (you will have to read it yourself to get to that bit), we go through the dark night of the senses. The dark night of the senses is what John calls 'purgative contemplation'. It is a path which we can take after discovering that we have formed attachments, as Meister Eckhart speaks of above. John tells us that 'the night of purgative contemplation had lulled to sleep and mortified, in the house of sensuality, all passions and desires, in their rebellious movements'.[8] It is a time of our inner self being cleansed by the Divine and drawn deeper into the contemplative path.

This is not a comfortable situation. John of the Cross says:

> Souls begin to enter the dark night of the senses when God is drawing them out of the state of beginners, which is that of those who meditate on the spiritual road, and is leading them into that of proficient, the state of contemplatives, that, having passed through it, they may arrive at the state of perfect, which is that of the divine union with God.[9]

But perhaps we are not aware that we are at this stage and that the Divine is drawing us through it. Perhaps all we are aware of is the darkness surrounding us. We may think that we are doing well in our contemplative life, that we are progressing along the path with speed, or at least smoothly. This can, John says, bring about secret pride in our own selves. This is a mistake many beginners make, John says, and so when the Divine begins to lead them through the dark night of the senses, through purgative contemplation, they begin to fall into the mistaken idea that things are going badly, that they are failing in their contemplation, that somehow things are going wrong. But this is not the case. We each must, in our soul, be cleansed if we are to go further into and deeper into the Divine presence.

So perhaps we might feel that we are in a time of desolation in our contemplation, when in fact we are being drawn 'further up and further in', as C.S. Lewis says in *The Last Battle*. Perhaps we have been called to step into a deeper state of being and the Divine is taking us through the dark night of the senses. Seek refuge in the Divine presence within to discover whether this is the case.

An empty void in prayer

Finally, and not too dissimilarly, I want to look at something which the 20th-century Jesuit priest Anthony DeMello talks of: the dark empty void we face when we begin along the contemplative path. Having spoken about removing our concepts and images of the Divine (see chapter 6), DeMello speaks of contemplation as a loving gaze into the eyes of Ultimate Love. But if we have removed all of our images of the Divine, what do we gaze into? 'An imageless, formless reality. A blank!'[10]

But most people struggle with this. They feel that there is nothing in this blank. But this is what is required of practitioners to go deeper into contemplation and deeper into the Divine Reality. In this silence and darkness, and staring into a blank, DeMello says that people have two cognitive reactions – one is to fall into the trap of starting verbal prayer again, and the other is to give up completely because you feel that you are doing nothing and that God is not there.

When people fall into the trap of reverting to verbal prayer, DeMello says, 'If God is gracious to them, and he very frequently is, he will make it impossible for them to use their mind in prayer… Vocal prayer will be unbearable to them because the words seem meaningless; they will just go dry.'[11] Have you ever felt like your words in prayer are useless? That they are just falling to the floor when they leave your mouth or hitting the ceiling instead of penetrating heaven? Perhaps that is because God is wanting you to stop using words and be drawn into the deeper way of silence. We may feel this emptiness consuming us, this empty dark void engulfing us, and so feel that the Divine is absent. However, as DeMello continues:

> If they… persevere in the exercise of [silent] prayer and expose themselves, in blind faith, to the emptiness, the idleness, the darkness, the nothingness, they will gradually discover, at first in small flashes, later in a more permanent fashion, that there is a glow in the darkness, that the emptiness mysteriously fills their heart, that the idleness is full of God's activity, that in the nothingness their being is recreated and shaped anew.[12]

Similarly to John of the Cross' dark night of the senses, DeMello expresses this idea that the Divine draws us deliberately through a dark void, as this is the only way into a deeper experience of the deep silence found at the heart of the Divine.

If we are feeling that we are in a time of desolation, perhaps we have been called to step into a deeper state of being and the Divine is taking us through the dark empty void, which is actually filled with the luminous activity of the Divine. We are at the point of staring blankly into the nothingness, so we feel nothing. Seek refuge in the Divine presence within to discover whether this is the case. There is a picture which frequently passes by my social media newsfeed which reflects this. It is of a seed planted in the ground with a picture next to it of shoots growing. It has words around it which say, 'If you feel that you are in a dark confined place, then perhaps you have been planted because you are ready to grow.' Wait. Don't immediately despair. Discover why you feel this way by seeking the Divine.

In our times of consolation, we create the inner environment to connect with the Divine within ourselves, so that we can, in our times of desolation, walk that path even when it seems dark and void. It is in these times of trial that we test the reality of the faith we say we have in times of ease.

God is our refuge and our strength, an ever-present help in times of trouble. The Divine is within us, and we can draw on that Divine presence within our own inner being and take refuge there. Even when we feel that there is an absence, we can be sure that the Divine presence will never leave us nor forsake us.

Find sanctuary in the Divine presence dwelling within you. Sit comfortably in that inner sacred space, no matter what is going on in your life, no matter the desolation you feel you are going through. Be confident that the Divine is there and is your refuge and strength in all things and at all times.

11

Natural space

The authentic Christian mystic is notoriously earthy. He loves the earth and takes good care of it. He remains as poor as possible so that he can leave many earthly things unused, and therefore unspoiled by human greed. He recognizes how sacramental the earth is… He sees everything as a sign, sample, or symbol of God and therefore he affirms the totality of being.

William McNamara[1]

The surrounding natural world has been the place of worship and connection with the Divine for a lot longer than religious groups have been meeting inside buildings. Sadly, because of 1,700 years of dualistic theology pumped into the western church by the Latin Fathers, much of western Christianity has a huge blind spot when it comes to eco-theology and experiencing the Divine in and through the natural world, and may even wrongly think that that sort of thing is pagan and has no place in Christianity.

Contrarywise, the Eastern Orthodox Church, uninfluenced by the Latin church Fathers, has care for creation and the engagement with the Divine in and through the natural world as core aspects of its theology. In the study notes to Genesis 1, the Orthodox Study Bible says:

The repeated affirmation 'and God saw that it was good' in Genesis 1 underscores the intrinsic, fundamental *goodness* of matter and the whole created order, even after the Fall. This understanding is the basis for a sacramental world view – that the created order not only is good, but also can be a means of communion with God... Moreover, the astounding beauty, intricate order, and sublime harmony of all aspects of creation, as well as the tremendously vast expanse of the universe, are intended to draw mankind to an awareness of and appreciation for the Creator.[2]

The head of the Eastern Orthodox Church, His All Holiness Ecumenical Patriarch Bartholomew, says:

An Orthodox Christian perspective on the natural environment derives from the fundamental belief that the world was created by a loving God... The entire world contains seeds and traces of the Living God... If the earth is sacred then our relationship with the natural environment is mystical and sacramental... Each plant, each animal, and each microorganism tells a story, unfolds a mystery, relates an extraordinary harmony and balance, which are interdependent and complimentary... The same dialogue of communication and mystery of communication is detected in the galaxies, where the countless stars betray the same mystical beauty and mathematical interconnectedness... The coexistence and correlation between the boundlessly infinite and the most insignificantly finite things articulate a concelebration of joy and love. This is precisely what the seventh century Saint Maximus the Confessor called a 'cosmic liturgy'... [Everything is] *a part* of the universe, and cannot be considered or conceived *apart* from the universe. In this way the natural environment ceases to be something that we observe objectively and exploit selfishly, and becomes a part of the 'cosmic liturgy' or celebration of the essential interconnection and interdependence of all things.[3]

The natural world is not just the backdrop for the activity of humanity; it is not just a resource centre to enable us to live as comfortably and easily as possible; it is an interconnected symbiotic organism with which we are intricately interwoven as a part. As the saying goes, whatever we do to the earth, we ultimately do to ourselves.[4] As Bede Griffiths says:

> The physical universe is a web of interdependent relationships. There is nothing in the world that is not dependent in some way upon everything else. This is affirmed by modern science… Through meditation we discover and uncover our links with the whole creation. We put ourselves into harmony with the universe and integrate ourselves with all humanity.[5]

Care for creation is intricately interwoven with our spiritual reality and the Christ-centred life we live. In fact, it is not possible to be an authentic Christian if we do not love that which God loves, and God loves the entire created order so much that it is a reason Christ came and died on the cross. John 3:16 tells us that 'God so loved the world.' The word 'world' in English translations in the original Greek is *kosmos*, from which we get the English word 'cosmos'.

When we think of the cosmos, we generally think of space, but in the original Greek it meant the entire created order, everything which has been made. As I grew up in a conservative evangelical cocoon, it was impressed upon me that John 3:16 was a verse which said that God loved me, and all of humanity, so much that Jesus died for me. You may have been taught this same interpretation of this verse. But this anthropocentric misinterpretation removes the grander and deeper reality and joy of what John was actually saying. It wasn't just for humanity that Jesus died, and it wasn't just because God loved me and human beings; it was because God loved the *kosmos* – the whole of creation, the stars and planets, the trees and flowers, the animals and birds, the fish and minibeasts (yes, even the spiders which get in your bathtub and the wasps that join you on your summer picnics!) – that Christ died.

This links in with statements which the apostle Paul makes about the sacredness of creation. He tells us:

> The creation was subjected to futility, not of its own will but by the will of the one who subjected it, in hope that the creation itself will be set free from its bondage to decay and will obtain the freedom of the glory of the children of God. We know that the whole creation has been groaning in labour pains until now.
> ROMANS 8:20–22 (NRSV)

And later on Paul tells us that 'God was pleased... to reconcile to himself *all things*, whether things on earth or things in heaven, by making peace through his blood, shed on the cross' (Colossians 1:19–20, emphasis mine). The work of the cross was not just about humanity; it was a work of reconciliation for the whole of creation, to draw all of creation back into a relationship with the creator. Both the apostles John and Paul tell us that there is something more to the natural world for the Divine than it just being a 'thing' that was created. They express the idea that there is a relationship between all of creation and the creator, and that it is all loved and will all be reconciled. The work of the cross is not just for humans, but for everything you see (and don't see); this is how much the Divine loves the natural world (including you), so therefore this should be the foundation of our own attitude towards the natural world.

This is ultimately expressed by Jesus' command to 'go into all the world and preach the gospel to all creation' (Mark 16:15) – literally, to all that has been created. Francis of Assisi took this literally, as he did when he heard the Divine voice telling him to rebuild his church, and he preached to the birds and the fish. But my understanding of preaching the gospel goes beyond the words which we say to others. To preach the gospel holistically includes the way we behave, the actions we make, the life we live. As the saying goes, which is often erroneously attributed to Francis: 'Preach the gospel all the time, and if necessary, use words.' So to preach the gospel to all creation means to act towards it in a way which expresses the gospel of Christ – the good news of love and reconciliation with the creator.

But for mystics, modern and past, it is not just about eco-theology and how we treat the planet, as important as they are, but it is also about how we can encounter and engage with the Divine in and through the natural world. It is about having mystical, transcendent experiences of the Divine in and through nature.

In his book about Forest Church, the rapidly growing movement that he co-founded, Bruce Stanley tells a story of him having a transcendent experience with the Divine while out on his mountain bike early one spring morning in the forest. He tells how, for some years now, he has been asking people to describe where they had their most transcendent experience with the Divine, or where they felt the barrier between the physical and spiritual was 'thinnest'. 'The majority of people's descriptions of these,' he says, 'are from nature (I've yet to hear many descriptions of these occurring during religious services in buildings)... Nature is a doorway into the other-than-human world which is more than plants and animals. It reveals secrets about its Creator, and it's somewhere God can speak to us; nature is sacred space.'[6]

The apostle Paul, once again, can help us set a foundation for what we are about to unfold. He tells us that 'by taking a long and thoughtful look at what God has created, people have always been able to see what their eyes as such can't see: eternal power, for instance, and the mystery of his divine being' (Romans 1:20, MSG). According to the apostle Paul, we can encounter the mystery of the Divine being in and through the natural world.

The natural world is saturated with the Divine presence, the Divine energy and essence flow through the natural world. Everything has an essence of the Divine within it. When we look at it, we can see the mystery of the Divine being. This is not about looking at something and pulling a sermon illustration or a lesson out of it; this is about actually encountering the Divine in the trees and rocks, in the sunset and the seashore. It is about taking a walk in a natural environment and bumping into God.

In the 14th century, Meister Eckhart, whom we met in an earlier chapter, once said that every creature is a word of God, and that if he could spend enough time with one tiny creature, even a caterpillar, he would never have to preach another sermon (it is worth noting here that the Dominican Order, of which Eckhart was a high standing member, is known as the Order of Preachers). So full of God is each creature, even a caterpillar, that the observer would be so filled and saturated with that Divine presence flowing through it, that all words would cease to be necessary. 'For before there were creatures,' Eckhart says, 'God was not "God": He was [simply] That which He was. But when creatures came into existence and received their created being, then God was not "God" in Himself – He was "God" in creatures.'[7]

A few centuries before Meister Eckhart, Hildegard of Bingen had many mystical visions. Some of these visions included what she called the *viriditas*. There is no direct English translation for this, and in the English translation of her works in which it is repeatedly found, it is translated using different words. But the general understanding is that what she saw was a green flowing energy which connected all things. It flowed between her and the trees and the rocks and the creatures, and it was this which connected everything and held everything together. This energy was the Divine presence in the natural world. I often jokingly call Hildegard the first Jedi, as the way she saw this *viriditas* sounds remarkably like how Yoda explains the Force to Luke Skywalker as he trains him!

This *viriditas*, I believe, can be expanded into what today is called quantum consciousness or quantum relationships, that is, the relations between seemingly separate things which are actually connected through a higher state of consciousness.

Let us start with some basics: our brains work at four different levels – we have beta brainwaves, which is the cognitive consciousness. You are using your beta brainwaves right now to read this book and process the words. It is what we use for thinking, and what has wrongly been placed as the most important part of our consciousness by the modern west. Then there are the alpha brainwaves. Alpha brainwaves are the ones which engage in daydreaming and imagining. They are what lots of inventions develop from. Third we have the theta brainwaves. Theta brainwaves are your subconscious. They are the ones which set things into your long-term memory and interact with the alpha waves in your dreams. Finally there are the delta brainwaves. Delta brainwaves are what some call our higher consciousness, that which enables us to connect with the transcendent and to feel connected with something 'more'. This is the connection with quantum consciousness – our connection with all things. For let us remember that consciousness is not something that is only in humans.

'Consciousness is not a human phenomenon; nor does it pertain to the human brain alone,' says Ilia Delio. She continues:

> By understanding brain activity in light of quantum physics, we have come to understand consciousness as a cosmic pheno-menon... Quantum relationships create something new by drawing together things that were initially separate and indi-vidual... The quantum world is a continuous dance of energy in which relationships form reality... Two quantum particles that at one time interact and then move away from each other are for-ever bonded and act as though they were one thing regardless of the distance between them. The material world is non-local. If reality is non-local, that is, if things can affect one another despite distance or space-time coordinates, then nature is not composed of material substances, but deeply entangled fields of energy; the nature of the universe is undivided wholeness. Because our consciousness has emerged from this wholeness and continues to be part of it, then what accounts for the human mind is active in the universe.[8]

The brain is not the only place from where our neural pathways flow. There are neural centres in both our heart and our gut as well. This is why you 'feel' things in your heart or gut, because these neural path-ways are created from there.

> Our brains have been found to communicate with other parts of our body in ways which are surprising. Neurones in our stomach are now seen as a 'Second Brain', feeding back information to the central nervous system. More recently, the role of gut microbes has emerged. In the same way as trees are highly dependent on their microbial environment, our stomach microbes make chem-icals that affect the brain and influence the way that we feel or

function. The overall impression is that, rather like nature itself, parts of the body previously seen as separate are now regarded by scientists as interconnected.[9]

Our whole holistic being works together, but we have often been misguided into thinking that we should focus our internal 'training' on the beta brainwave, simply on cognitive knowledge and information. I believe that those who practise strengthening the delta brainwaves alongside the quantum consciousness, best done in my experience through contemplation, are those who connect most deeply with the collective unconscious and the Divine in all things, those we might call mystics.

It is through all of these things, especially the delta brainwaves and quantum consciousness, that we are able to connect deeply and transcendently with the natural world, in which there is also a consciousness – not just in animals, but in plants too. Through scientific research, we have discovered that trees particularly have a consciousness. They communicate with each other through the interwoven network of roots and use fungi to transmit information. We know that parent trees can identify which trees around them are their own offspring, and favour them in transferring information about nutrients in the soil. Deciduous trees also make a conscious decision as to when they start the abscission process (dropping their leaves in the autumn), and which leaves on which branches to drop in order to be most effective to their well-being.

We know that flowers communicate with bees to tell them whether or not there is any nectar in them, which is why bees will fly into some flowers, but hover at others and then fly away; they are 'listening' to the flower to find out whether it is worth going in.[10] There is a conscious awareness in all of creation, and this relates to the relationship that the whole of creation has with its Creator, and it is also something which we, as part of the natural creation, can tap into and through which we can experience the Divine in nature.

Nature can be perhaps the greatest sanctuary for our inner being, for our spiritual growth, for our deep transcendent connection with the Divine.

So I suggest you stop here. Put this book down, and go and walk in some part of nature, be it your back garden, a local park, a forest, a beach, a clifftop, a meadow, wherever – just go and walk and interact with the natural world. Turn your beta brainwaves off and tune into the delta brainwaves. Feel the natural world, both physically by touching it (go on! Go hug a tree!) and with your internal awareness in the neuro-centre in your heart. Become aware of its consciousness and of the Divine presence in which it is saturated. Become one with it through your pre-existing interconnection with it.

12

Contemplata aliis tradere

The great mystics tell us that the vision of God in his own light – the direct contact of the soul's substance with the Absolute... is the prelude, not to a further revelation of the eternal order given to you, but to an utter change, a vivid life springing up within you; which they sometimes call the 'transforming union'... by which you may first desire, then tend to, then achieve contact with Reality... [It] becomes strong and vigorous, invades and transmutes the whole personality, and makes of it, not a 'dreamy mystic' but an active and impassioned servant of the Eternal Wisdom.

Evelyn Underhill[1]

At the end of every workshop day or residential retreat which I run, I like to have a session where we look at how we might take what we have learned and implement it into our everyday life back in our normal worlds. It is all well and good to go away to a teaching day or retreat, or to read a spiritual book, but unless it makes a difference to who you are as a person, it has really only been a nice time and not transformative. Even if the transformation is very slight, or it is a seed planted which will take time to grow, or it is the fact that you might look at life or some aspect of it differently, then that is what you take away with you, and that makes a difference to you.

However, we must not forget, as we discovered in an earlier chapter, that this transformation is a continuing journey from our false self into our true self; it is a further discovery of who we truly are: 'The contemplative life is not about becoming someone different from who you are, but rather about being who you *really* are to begin with.'[2] This continued journey of discovery of your true self and deepening journey into the Divine presence, and this transformation of who you are, will be projected through your subconscious and general being, and passed on to others through the life you actively live, not just the words you say to them.

The title of this chapter, 'Contemplata aliis tradere', is a Latin phrase which means to pass on to others what we have gained in contemplation, and is one of the central tenets of the Dominican Order. It was exemplified by one of the most famous Dominicans, Thomas Aquinas (13th century), who asked in his writings what sort of religious life was best devoted to contemplation. He concluded that it was one devoted to activism, such as giving alms or attending the sick, a life in which elements of both contemplation and action were present. What Aquinas actually said was: *Sicut enim maius est illuminare quam lucere solum, ita maius est contemplata aliis tradere quam solum contemplari* – which means, 'As it is better to illuminate than to shine only, so it is better to hand down to others the fruits of contemplation than to contemplate only.'[3] What we do should directly flow from what we gain from our contemplation.

We begin with contemplation, we begin by setting aside time, sitting in the silence and soaking in the Divine presence, as we have seen possible in myriad ways throughout this book. But that in itself, and its continued practise, should not just be a nice time which brings us a lovely sense of inner calm. Rather, it should transform our inner being, as Evelyn Underhill says in the quotation above. This causes us to shift from someone who practises contemplation and contemplative techniques, into *being* a contemplative. It becomes something ontological rather than cerebral. It becomes a part of our being, a part of who we are as a person, and that in turn is passed on through the transformed life that we begin to live. William McNamara says:

> The effectiveness of a man's apostolic work [what God sends him out to do] depends upon the reality and intensity of his mystical life [the personal experiential encounters with the Divine]. No one can give what they do not have. One silent, solitary, God-centred, God-intoxicated man can do more to keep God's love alive and his presence felt in the world than a thousand half-hearted, talkative, busy men living frightened, fragmented lives of quiet desperation.[4]

Meister Eckhart said that through our contemplative practice we can become so filled with the Divine presence that we cannot help but pour that out in a life of action. For him, one thing naturally led to the other. The Jesuits, founded by Ignatius of Loyola in the 16th century, had a similar thought. The Jesuits thought themselves to exist as *actione contemplativi*, contemplatives in action:[5]

> While Ignatius counselled his Jesuits always to carve out time for prayer, they were expected to lead active lives… they were to be active people who adopted a contemplative, or meditative, stance toward the world… By being [fully] aware of the world around us – in the midst of activity – we can allow a contemplative stance to inform our actions. Instead of seeing the spiritual [monastic] life as one that exists only if it is enclosed by the walls of a monastery, Ignatius asks you to see the world as your monastery.[6]

This is also why Richard Rohr's centre has the name it does. Rohr is a modern-day mystic and a First Order Franciscan, more recently taking on more of a hermit life. The centre he founded in America is called the Centre for Action and Contemplation. Their website says,

> The name was chosen because it expressed the paradoxical nature of the Center's purpose: standing in a middle place, at the center of the cross, where opposites are held together. We believed that action and contemplation, once thought of as mutually exclusive, must be brought together or neither one would make sense. Richard Rohr founded the 'Center for Action and Contemplation' in 1987 because he saw a deep need for the integration of both action and contemplation – the two are inseparable. As Father Richard likes to say, the most important word in our Center's name is neither Action nor Contemplation, but the word and. Contemplation is a way of listening with the heart while not relying entirely on the head. Contemplation is a prayerful letting go of our sense of control and choosing to cooperate with God and God's work in the world. Prayer without action, as Father Richard says, can promote our tendency to self-preoccupation, and without contemplation, even well-intended actions can cause more harm than good.[7]

So how might what you have read in this book change the way you live your life? How has it already helped the ongoing transformation into your true self which you are living?

In the Ignatian tradition, also known as the Jesuits – the Friends of Jesus – started by Ignatius of Loyola, mentioned above, there is a practice called the Examen. In this practice one looks back to see where the Divine presence was and where the Divine was influencing you along the way. Usually this is done mentally looking back over the day. While

Ignatius is known to have had his monks do this twice a day, once in the middle to look back at the morning period and once at night to look back over the afternoon period, I want to suggest that you pause here and do a literary Examen. Look back over this book, and any notes you might have made relating to it, any pages you have marked or folded over, and just see where the Divine presence was and what the Divine was saying to you as you journeyed through it. Stop now, but don't put the book down. Go back to the parts through which the Divine spoke to you the most and revisit what that still, small voice whispered into your being.

For the final time, welcome back to the book. Or at least, to the continued reading of it.

I want to look now at balance. Balance is key to the universe, and also to you. Heraclitus, the Greek philosopher, said that all things are held together through the tension of opposites. It is the balance of the life force between opposites which keeps the universe going. Interestingly, Heraclitus used the Greek word *logos* to describe the tension between opposites which holds the universe together (the same Greek word, translated 'Word', is used in John 1 to describe Jesus).

For Benedict balance was essential – and indeed for the whole monastic tradition. Balance is key. We must get the balance right between 'being' and 'doing', not emphasise one to the detriment of the other.

Unfortunately, in our modern western culture doing is seen as much more important than being. We are judged, and we judge others (albeit subconsciously), by what we and they do, and how well it is done. It is so ingrained into our psyche that we don't even realise that we do it. It is pretty much the first thing we ask of someone when we first meet them. 'Hello, what's your name?' The answer comes, then, 'And what do you do?' There it is! That imbalance. That judgement. As soon as we hear the answer, our subconscious will determine whether we think this person is 'worthy' or not.

We are also judged on how effective we are in what we do. If one person is more productive in what they do than someone else who does the same thing, they are deemed better. We judge people by what they do, how much they do and whether or not we think it is worthwhile to do it.

However, 'being', or intentionally doing nothing (which is different to finding yourself with nothing to do), is not so well thought of. In fact, it could be seen as wasting time, as though we feel we should be getting on with something.

There is a wonderful Chinese proverb, often attributed to Lao Tzu, as most generic Chinese proverbs are, which says, 'I meditate for one hour every morning, unless I am very busy and have much to do, then I meditate for two hours.' If we have more to 'do', then we need to 'be' more as well.

Balance is the key. Balance between being and doing. Both are important, both should be done and both should be seen as equal in their significance to life. The more you have to do, the more you should be – that is the moral of the Chinese proverb. I believe that it is this balance which the author of the book of James was trying to get across when they spoke of faith and works (see James 2:14–18). They need to be in balance – faith and works, being and doing.

The following is an edited version of an article about balance which I wrote in 2010 for the quarterly magazine of the Community of Aidan and Hilda:

One of the things that we commit to as members of the Community of Aidan and Hilda is to keep our lives in a rhythm. Rhythm and balance are very closely linked, as there cannot be a good rhythm if things are out of balance. At Spring Harvest this year, we were asked to give an interview on living by a Way of Life in one of the seminars that Russ Rook was leading. Our Members Guardian braved the first session, and I the second. The last thing that Russ asked me was that if there was one thing I would say was the key to living a Way of Life, what would it be? I replied that I believe balance to be the answer; to have things in balance was key to living a Way of Life.

Recently I had a question for God, something which I was struggling with. My usual way to deal with this is to go and spend time with the Divine out in creation, dwell in the Divine presence for a while and allow the Divine voice to soak into my heart. So this was exactly what I did. The question I had was this: 'Why is it that I can have such inner peace within me one moment and be attuned to the Divine voice, but then another, not?' This was bothering me, so I wandered for a while in creation near where I live, along the banks of a river among the trees, watching the birds and fish along the way.

As I walked, I came across a tree which had a branch that drooped down and then up again in a curve a bit like a hammock, just low enough in its droop for me to sit on the branch. As I sat on the branch with my feet on the floor and closed my eyes to spend some time in contemplative meditation, I felt the need to sit cross-legged as I did this. I looked at the ground to see where I might be able to sit, when I felt the Divine voice in my heart say, 'Stay on the branch.' *Cross-legged?* I thought. I looked at the branch. It was not very wide, but I thought I would give it a go, so I hoisted myself up on to the branch. It took some time, a few attempts and quite some effort, and a lot of help from the walking staff I always take with me, but I managed to get myself on to the branch cross-legged. For some time I continued to use the staff resting on the ground to balance me, but then felt I should remove the staff from the ground and place it across my lap, as I usually do when in this position. This too took a few attempts, and a few more times of ending up on the ground again, but I managed to do it.

So there I was, sitting cross-legged on the branch with no support, only my balance to keep me there. I was feeling quite pleased with myself. However, a quiet and gentle gust of wind (Divinely sent, I am sure) made the branch bounce and sway a little, and I lost my balance again. Quickly moving the staff from its place and pushing it against the ground, I regained my balance without falling from the branch. I placed the staff back across my lap and continued to sit cross-legged on the branch, doing well with my balance (continuing to be quite impressed with myself).

Then I decided to continue in my contemplative meditation while on the branch, and so I closed my eyes to listen to the outer and inner sounds. This proved to be a mistake. With my eyes open I could balance (pretty well), but as soon as I closed my eyes I seemed to lose all ability to balance at all! Numerous times the staff was swung from its place to the ground, and once or twice I ended up on the ground again myself.

Then God spoke (after laughing to himself while watching me, I should imagine). He taught me that there is a difference between *ob*taining balance and *main*taining balance. I was quite good at obtaining balance, quietness and inner stillness in life, but to maintain this balance throughout the whole of life, every day, with all that I would have to deal with, was a whole other thing altogether. Although I have learned and am well practised at how to obtain balance and inner stillness, it is how to maintain this balance that I must learn, and which he has continued to teach me in the days which have followed.

Thankfully, over the past ten years or so, I have continued to receive from this lesson, and I find I am much better at maintaining that balance while in every place and in every situation.

Thomas Merton said that the contemplative's life was 'a prolonged immersion in the rivers of tranquillity that flow from God into the whole universe and draw all things back into God'.[8]

In our contemplative practices we obtain balance. The Divine work within us, transforming us into our true selves, enables us to maintain that balance, and in doing so we are able to project the Divine peace into the world, in which we are called to live and move and have our being. We pass on to others what we have gained in contemplation not just by telling people, but also by the way we live our lives, by the way we express ourselves, by the way we approach life, by the way we deal with the difficulties and pressures, and by the way we embody Divine peace. We become better reflections of the Divine glory as the Divine Spirit works in us (2 Corinthians 3:18) and so we begin to transform the world – peace in ourselves, peace in the world!

A blessing of Divine peace be upon you:
A blessing of stillness rest upon your being.
A blessing of silence fill your being.
A blessing of solitude be in your being.
A blessing of sanctuary surround your being.

Notes

Introduction

1 Boniface Ramsey, *John Cassian: The Conferences (Ancient Christian Writers Series No. 57)* (Newman Press, 1997), p. 331.

2 Found in a letter from Hidegard to Odo of Soissons, in 1148 (known as Letter 40R). This comes from the fuller quote: 'Listen: there was once a king sitting on his throne. Around him stood great and wonderfully beautiful columns ornamented with ivory, bearing the banners of the king with great honour. Then it pleased the king to raise a small feather from the ground and he commanded it to fly. The feather flew, not because of anything in itself but because the air bore it along. So am I "a feather on the breath of God".'

3 Jaroslav Jan Pelikan Jr., *The Vindication of Tradition: The 1983 Jefferson lecture in the humanities* (Yale University Press, 1986).

4 Joseph Carey, 'Christianity as an enfolding circle: conversation with Jaroslav Pelikan', *US News and World Report*, 26 June 1989, p. 57.

5 Carl McColman, *Christian Mystics: 108 seers, saints, and sages* (Hampton Road Press, 2016).

6 **aidanandhilda.org.uk**

7 Thomas Merton, *New Seeds of Contemplation* (Shambala Publications, 2003), p. 270.

8 From her thirteenth Revelation of Divine Love.

9 **pursuitofsilence.com**

10 Martin Laird, *Into the Silent Land: The practice of contemplation* (DLT, 2006).

1 Slowing down

1 Evelyn Underhill, *Light of Christ: Addresses given at the House of Retreat Pleshey, in May, 1932* (Longmans, Green and Co, 1944), pp. 105–106.

2 The dictionary definition of a mystic is one who uses contemplative practices to become of one mind and will with their deity. There is nothing un-Christian about being a mystic.

3 Thomas Merton, *New Seeds of Contemplation* (Shambala Publications, 2003), pp. 1–2.

4 See, for example, my book *The Mystic Path of Meditation: Beginning a Christ-centred journey* (Anamchara Books, 2013) or **insighttimer.com/davidcole**.

5 Cole, *The Mystic Path of Meditation*, pp. 54–58.

6 Cole, *The Mystic Path of Meditation*, p. 14.

7 Underhill, *Light of Christ*, pp. 102–103.

8 You can either find a centre which has a programme of retreats – **retreats.org.uk/findaretreat.php** – or discover particular retreat leaders and see what they are doing – for example, **waymarkministries.com/retreats.html**.

9 Two good starting points are Ian Bradley, *Pilgrimage: A spiritual and cultural journey* (Lion, 2009) and Andrew Jones, *Every Pilgrim's Guide to Celtic Britain and Ireland* (Canterbury Press, 2002).

10 A great simple resource and introduction to labyrinths is Brian Draper, *Labyrinth: Illuminating the inner path* (Lion Hudson, 2010).

2 Be still and know

1 Mother Julian of Norwich (edited by Halcyon Backhouse and Rhona Pipe), *Revelations of Divine Love: Thirteenth revelation* (Hodder Publishing, 2009), p. 90.

2 'Mantra' is a Sanskrit word which denotes a word or short phrase used to aid focus and meditation. Literally the word means 'instrument of thought'.

3 **insighttimer.com/davidcole/guided-meditations/be-still-and-know-i-am-god-2**

4 Thomas Merton, *New Seeds of Contemplation* (Shambala Publications, 2003), pp. 36–37.

5 Merton, *New Seeds of Contemplation*, p. 37.

6 Merton, *New Seeds of Contemplation*, p. 37.

7 Merton, *New Seeds of Contemplation*, p. 36.

8 Merton, *New Seeds of Contemplation*, p. 42.

9 Mother Julian of Norwich, *Revelations of Divine Love*, p. 92.

10 Silvana Panciera (translated by Piero Giogi and Bernard Delcourt), *The Beguines: Women in search of sanctity within freedom* (Insertion Press, 2014), p. 72.

3 Still here

1 Brother Lawrence, *The Practice of the Presence of God and Spiritual Maxims* (Dover Publications, 2005), p. 16.
2 **en.wikipedia.org/wiki/Mindfulness**
3 Thich Nhat Hanh, *The Miracle of Mindfulness* (Rider Publishing, 1991), pp. 14–15.
4 *Kung Fu Panda*, dir. John Stevenson, Mark Osborne (DreamWorks Animation, 2008), 30m53s.
5 Anthony DeMello, *Awareness* (Zondervan, 2002), pp. 37–38.
6 St Gregory Palamas, *The Triads (Classics of Western Spirituality series)* (Paulist Press, 1983), pp. 45–46.
7 Lawrence, *The Practice of the Presence of God and Spiritual Maxims*, p. 3.
8 Lawrence, *The Practice of the Presence of God and Spiritual Maxims*, p. 15.
9 Lawrence, *The Practice of the Presence of God and Spiritual Maxims*, p. 16.
10 Lawrence, *The Practice of the Presence of God and Spiritual Maxims*, pp. 53–54.
11 Carmen Acevedo Butcher (trans.), *The Cloud of Unknowing* (Shambala Publications, 2009), p. 85.
12 John Climacus. *The Ladder of Divine Perfection* (Holy Transfiguration Monastery, Massachusetts, 1982), p. 194.
13 *The Cloud of Unknowing*, pp. 85–87.
14 Thomas Keating, *Intimacy with God: An introduction to Centring Prayer* (The Crossroad Publishing Company, 2009), p. 29.

4 In pursuit of silence

1 Maggie Ross, *Silence: A user's guide* (DLT, 2017), p. 40.
2 Ross, *Silence*, p. 101.
3 *In Pursuit of Silence*, dir. Patrick Shen (Transcendental Media, 2016): **pursuitofsilence.com**.
4 *Quaker Faith and Practice, fifth edition* (The Yearly Meeting of the Religious Society of Friends (Quakers) in Britain, 2013), section 2.12.

5 Into the silent land

1 Martin Laird, *Into the Silent Land: The practice of contemplation* (DLT, 2006), p. 3.
2 **aidanandhilda.org.uk**
3 **etymonline.com**
4 John of the Cross, 'Maxims on love' in Kieran Kavanaugh and Otilio Rodriguez (trans.) *The Collected Works of St John of the Cross* (ICS Publications, 1991), p. 675.
5 Laird, *Into the Silent Land*, pp. 23–24.
6 Teresa of Ávila, *Interior Castle* (Ave Maria Press, 2007), p. 43.
7 Teresa of Ávila, *Interior Castle*, p. 42.
8 Laird, *Into the Silent Land*, p. 3.
9 David Cole, *The Mystic Path of Meditation: Beginning a Christ-centred journey* (Anamchara Books, 2013), pp. 65–80.
10 Bede Griffiths, *The Universal Christ: Daily readings with Bede Griffiths* (DLT, 1990), p. 16.
11 Found in the *Russian Orthodox Prayer Book* (Printshop of Saint Job of Pochaev, 2019), p. 400.
12 *Russian Orthodox Prayer Book*, p. 401.
13 His All Holiness Ecumenical Patriarch Bartholomew, *Encountering the Mystery: Understanding Orthodox Christianity today* (Doubleday Press, 2008), pp. 80–81.

6 The wordless way

1 Mark McIntosh, *Mystical Theology: The integrity of spirituality and theology* (Blackwell Publishers, 1998).
2 For more on this, you can find the video recordings for the teaching of a retreat I co-led on the subject with Justin Coutts of New Eden Ministry here: **neweden.teachable.com/p/apophatic**
3 **sarum.ac.uk**
4 Taken from 'Treatise of the One God: How God is known by us', found in the *Suma Theologica* by Thomas Aquinas.
5 Richard Woods, *Eckhart's Way* (Veritas Publications, 2009); with related verses found in John 1:18; 5:37; 6:46; 1 John 4:20.
6 'The mystical theology' in Pseudo-Dionysius, *The Complete Works* (Paulist Press, 1987), p. 138.
7 **goodreads.com/author/quotes/182763.Michelangelo_Buonarroti**

8 Maurice O'C Walshe (trans.), *The Complete Mystical Works of Meister Eckhart* (Crossroad Publishing Company, 2009), sermon 22.

9 *The Complete Mystical Works of Meister Eckhart*, sermon 51.

10 Louise Nelstrop, *Christian Mysticism: An introduction to contemporary theoretical approaches* (Ashgate Publishing, 2009), p. 95.

11 *The Complete Mystical Works of Meister Eckhart*, sermon 54.

12 Oliver Davies, *Meister Eckhart: Mystical theologian* (SPCK, 2011), p. 115.

13 Peter Rollins, *How (Not) to Speak of God: Marks of the emerging church* (SPCK, 2006), p. 19.

14 Michael A. Sells, *Mystical Languages of Unsaying* (University of Chicago Press, 1994).

15 *Concise Oxford English Dictionary* (Oxford University Press, 1995).

16 Anthony DeMello, *Awareness* (Zondervan, 2002), pp. 124–25.

17 McIntosh, *Mystical Theology*.

18 Pseudo-Dionysius, 'The mystical theology'.

19 William James, *The Varieties of Religious Experience: A study in human nature*.

20 McIntosh, *Mystical Theology*.

7 Go to your cell

1 Christopher C. Moore, *Solitude: A neglected path to God* (Cowley Publications, 2001), p. 15.

2 *Hashem* is used in the Jewish translation of Old Testament instead of any direct name of God, especially YHWH. It literally means 'the name'.

3 This version from Benedicta Ward, *The Desert Fathers: Sayings of the early Christian monks* (Penguin Classics, 2003), p. 10.

4 'Letter of Jerome to Marcella', in Joan M. Peterson, *Handmaids of the Lord: Contemporary descriptions of feminine asceticism in the first six Christian centuries* (Cistercian Publications, 1996), p. 106.

5 Laura Swan, *The Forgotten Desert Mothers: Sayings, lives, and stories of early Christian women* (Paulist Press, 2001), p. 74.

6 Teresa of Ávila, *The Way of Perfection* (Kindle edition), p. 583.

7 **ecosia.org/images?q=Sadhu+Amar+Bharati**

8 Charles Wycliffe Goodwin (trans.), *The Anglo-Saxon Version of the Life of St Guthlac, Hermit of Crowland* (Leopold Classics publishing, reprint; originally published 1858), p. 19.

9 Moore, *Solitude*, p. 15.

10 Moore, *Solitude*, p. 15.

8 The desert of your heart

1 Thomas Merton, *The Wisdom of the Desert* (New Directions Press, 1970), pp. 3–4.
2 Merton, *The Wisdom of the Desert*, pp. 5, 14.
3 Laura Swan, *The Forgotten Desert Mothers: Sayings, lives, and stories of early Christian women* (Paulist Press, 2001), p. 31.
4 Swan, *The Forgotten Desert Mothers*, p. 31.

9 Alone together

1 Dietrich Bonhoeffer, *Life Together* (SCM Press, 2015), pp. 78, 89.
2 Laura Swan, *The Forgotten Desert Mothers: Sayings, lives, and stories of early Christian women* (Paulist Press, 2001), p. 127.
3 **etymonline.com/search?q=monk**
4 Leonard J. Doyle (trans.), *St Benedict's Rule for Monasteries* (Liturgical Press, 1950), p. 7.
5 Esther de Waal, *Seeking God: The way of St Benedict* (Collins Fount Press, 1990), pp. 84–85.
6 John O'Donohue, *Eternal Echoes: Exploring our hunger to belong* (Bantam Books, 2000), p. xvi.
7 The Northumbria Community, *Celtic Daily Prayer, Book 1* (Harper Collins, 1999), p. 167.
8 *Quaker Faith and Practice, fifth edition* (The Yearly Meeting of the Religious Society of Friends (Quakers) in Britain, 2013), section 2.17 and 2.14.
9 Craig Gardiner, *Melodies of a New Monasticism: Bonhoeffer's vision, Iona's witness* (SCM Press, 2018), p. 89.
10 Graham Cray, Ian Mobsby and Aaron Kennedy (eds), *New Monasticism as Fresh Expression of Church* (Canterbury Press, 2010), pp. 140–41.
11 See Phyllis Tickle, *The Great Emergence: How Christianity is changing and why (Baker Books, 2008)* for more on this.
12 See my blog at **waymarkministries.com/blog/the-world-is-my-monastery**.
13 Bonhoeffer, *Life Together*, pp. 78, 89.
14 For a fuller expansion, see our Community book, *New Celtic Monasticism for Everyday People: A pilgrim way*, by our Founding Guardian Ray Simpson.

10 Seeking refuge

1 Psalm 46:1, 7. 'Elohim' is the plural of 'El', which means 'God'. Elohim, therefore suggests a plurality to the One God of the Hebrews. This could point towards the Trinity, which Christians believe is the One God. 'YHWH', pronounced 'Y'Hovah', was the Jewish 'full name' of God, the God who introduced himself to Moses. 't'shaw-baw' is often translated as 'of hosts', and suggests some form of army, and so a good translation of 'YHWH t'shaw-baw' would be the 'Great God of the Heavenly Armies'.

2 See **etymonline.com**.

3 Maurice O'C Walshe (trans.), *The Complete Mystical Works of Meister Eckhart* (Crossroad Publishing Company, 2009), sermon 87, p. 566.

4 *The Complete Mystical Works of Meister Eckhart*, p. 566.

5 *The Complete Mystical Works of Meister Eckhart*, p. 569.

6 *The Complete Mystical Works of Meister Eckhart*, pp. 572, 574.

7 Carmen Acevedo Butcher (trans.), *The Cloud of Unknowing* (Shambala Publications, 2009), chapter 20.

8 John of the Cross, *The Dark Night of the Soul* (Fount Press, 1995), p. 7.

9 John of the Cross, *The Dark Night of the Soul*, p. 9.

10 Anthony DeMello, *Sadhana: A Way to God: Christian exercises in Eastern form* (Doubleday Publishers, 1984), p. 30.

11 DeMello, *Sadhana: A Way to God*, p. 31.

12 DeMello, *Sadhana: A Way to God*, p. 31.

11 Natural space

1 William McNamara, *Earthy Mysticism: Contemplation and the life of passionate presence* (Crossroad Publishing, 1987), pp. ix–x.

2 *The Orthodox Study Bible* (Thomas Nelson Press, 2008), p. 2. Note here the deliberate contrary position to the Latin theology of 'original sin', a theology which leads to detachment from the physical world.

3 His All Holiness Ecumenical Patriarch Bartholomew, *Encountering the Mystery: Understanding Orthodox Christianity today* (Doubleday Press, 2008), pp. 91–94.

4 Often attributed to Chief Seattle, but may not have been him.

5 Bede Griffiths, *The Universal Christ: Daily readings with Bede Griffiths* (DLT, 1990), p. 3.

6 Bruce Stanley, *Forest Church: A field guide to nature connection for groups and individuals* (Mystic Christ Press, 2013), p. 18: **mysticchrist. co.uk/forest_church**.

7 Maurice O'C Walshe (trans.), *The Complete Mystical Works of Meister Eckhart* (Crossroad Publishing Company, 2009), p. 421.

8 Ilia Delio, *Making All Things New: Catholicity, cosmology, consciousness* (Orbis Books, 2020), pp. 58–62.

9 From a private conversation with Dr Lars Knutsen, neuroscience drug researcher. See also Emeran Mayer, *The Mind-Gut Connection: How the hidden conversation within our bodies impacts our mood, our choices, and our overall health* (HarperCollins, 2016).

10 All of this information can be found on various TED talks online from scientists.

12 Contemplata aliis tradere

1 Evelyn Underhill, *Practical Mysticism: A little book for normal people* (J.M. Dent & Sons Ltd Publishing, 1931), p. 151.

2 Carl McColman, *The Big Book of Christian Mysticism: The essential guide to contemplative spirituality* (Hampton Roads Publishing, 2010), p. 246.

3 Thomas Aquinus. *Suma Theologica II–II*, q. 188, article 6.

4 William McNamara OCD, *The Human Adventure* (Doubleday & Company Inc., 1974), p. 148.

5 See also **waymarkministries.com/blog/the-world-is-my-monastery**

6 James Martin, SJ., *The Jesuit Guide to (Almost) Everything: A spirituality for real life* (Harper Collins, 2010), p. 8.

7 **cac.org/about-cac/history**

8 Thomas Merton, *New Seeds of Contemplation* (Shambala Publications, 2003), p. 270.